Who Do Americans
Say That I Am?

Who Do Americans Say That I Am?

George Gallup, Jr.
and George O'Connell

The Westminster Press
Philadelphia

Scripture quotations are from *Good News Bible: The Bible in Today's English Version.* Old Testament: © American Bible Society, 1976; New Testament: © American Bible Society, 1966, 1971, 1976.

Book design by Gene Harris

First edition

Published by The Westminster Press®
Philadelphia, Pennsylvania

PRINTED IN THE UNITED STATES OF AMERICA

9 8 7 6 5 4 3 2

Library of Congress Cataloging-in-Publication Data

Gallup, George, 1930–
  Who do Americans say that I am?

  1. Jesus Christ—Person and offices—Public opinion. 2. Jesus Christ—Influence—Public opinion. 3. United States—Religion—Public opinion. 4. Public opinion—United States. I. O'Connell, George, 1923–   . II. Title.
BT205.G25 1986   232   85-26383
ISBN 0-664-24685-0 (pbk.)

Contents

Foreword
by Robert H. Schuller

I am a believer. I believe in God and his goodness. I also believe that he sent his Son, Jesus Christ, to earth to show us his way. And I believe that we are all God's children and therefore worthy of the redemption, happiness, and fulfillment that we can find through Jesus, both in the here-and-now and in the hereafter.

In a sixty-word nutshell, these are the essential beliefs that have shaped my life. They drew me to the ministry and impelled me to try to communicate my faith to others, both at the Crystal Cathedral and through the *Hour of Power* television ministry.

Many Americans share at least some of my views about Jesus. But how many, and why? And do his teachings and example really influence Americans' lives today?

I often asked these questions, of myself and others. I was seeking ways to be more effective, not only in enhancing and reinforcing the faith of my congregations but also in reaching out —to nonbelievers, to the skeptical and the wavering, and especially to the questing, those who would *like* to believe. To borrow a word from that wonderful musical comedy *The King and I,* it was a puzzlement.

During my long ministry, of course, I had gained many impressions of what Americans believe and how deeply these convictions affect their lives. Still, I couldn't really say that my impressions represented a true evaluation. Convincing the convinced or reinforcing their faith is a worthy and desirable objective, but how about the lost sheep? In Jesus' parable, the good shepherd sought out the one of the hundred that was lost and rejoiced when that one was found and rescued.

On the one hand, I could feel elated when I met someone whose life was enhanced by belief in Jesus. On the other, especially in my pastoral counseling, I got to understand the spiritual malaise and despair that a negative self-image and a lack of belief can engender. I knew that we must find better ways to spread the good news of Jesus.

Then my friend George Gallup, Jr., suggested that the answers to my puzzlement could best be found by determining, in considerable depth, just what Americans do feel about Jesus Christ. Questions could be posed to a representative cross-section of Americans in such a way that their deepest and truest feelings could be assessed. The Gallup Organization had conducted other surveys in recent years on subjects closely related to Christ's question, "Who do you say that I am?" As George put it, Jesus was both the messenger and the message. How Americans perceive him some two thousand years later could be a key to providing a more effective ministry.

It was an exciting idea. As co-chairman of The Gallup Organization, probably the best-known and most widely respected of the international polling organizations, George could provide objective data. He is himself a committed Christian and, equally important for our purposes, he is a skilled social scientist, whose findings and their interpretations on a wide variety of subjects provide guidelines for decision makers in business, politics, and industry, among others.

George and his associates at The Gallup Organization devised a series of carefully worded questions to be asked of a representative cross section of Americans.

Who was Jesus?

Was He God? Or was he just an inspired teacher, a Nazarene with charismatic appeal to a rebellious minority in the Roman empire?

Or was he God become man sent to redeem us as foretold in the Scriptures?

For nearly two thousand years, Jesus' ideas have persisted and influenced the world's history. Is this influence increasing, decreasing, or relatively unchanged today?

Do professed Christians actually practice what Jesus preached?

How many Americans would like to believe in Jesus but can't, for one reason or another?

These were not the actual questions, but they indicate the basic information we sought.

When assembled, the data seemed to create as many puzzlements as they answered. It became a matter of interpretation. George had cautioned us that the findings could be interpreted in several ways and that we would encounter anomalies.

We had to struggle with the data, but that was the glory of the exercise. It meant a lot of thinking and rethinking, which is always difficult. But it proved to be rewarding and revealing. I got a much clearer view of where we Americans stand in terms of our beliefs about Jesus and Christianity. The survey results also reinforced my hunch that organized religion has failed in its mission in many ways.

The data showed the classic "good-news, bad-news" formulation. The good news was that an overwhelming majority of Americans consider themselves Christians and feel that Jesus' teachings have influenced their lives. The bad news was that questions which went beneath the surface indicated that commitment to his teachings and example was considerably less than total.

We can accept the news media's fascination with the unusual, the "bad news" emphasis on departures from the norm. That's their business. But the fact remains that departures from the norm are just that: unusual. Still, Jesus' message of love, brotherhood, and forgiveness is not universally observed. I just wish it could be. I wish Americans would listen more closely to the message.

When George suggested that we should examine the study done for the Schuller Ministries, in light of other polls that his organization had done, I agreed readily. A better understanding by all Americans of other Americans' attitudes toward Jesus and Christianity could enrich us all.

This book is a result of that conviction. George Gallup enlisted the aid of George O'Connell, a writer whose convictions and writing style I admire, and together they have analyzed and interpreted the data. Their principal aim is to report the findings in an objective way. They also provide some historical perspective and insights into beliefs about Jesus and his impact on our lives. And they suggest some ways that Christians—both lay and clergy—can be more effective followers of Christ. I think they have succeeded on all counts.

Preface

Dr. Schuller has set forth the genesis and development of this book—our agreement that the findings of the Schuller Ministries studies, when combined with those of The Gallup Poll, the Princeton Religion Research Center, the U.S. Census Bureau, and other information and polling groups, could shed light on how Americans perceive Jesus and Christianity. From this material, Americans could achieve a better understanding of themselves and where they stand in relation to others in their beliefs and their commitment to religion.

Jesus enjoined his followers to "go, then, to all peoples everywhere and make them my disciples" (Matt. 28:19), and there is a strong evangelistic fervor among devoted Christians in the United States. Readers may see in the poll data what they want to see. But this is a mistake. The convictions of a narrow circle of family, friends, and co-religionists or statements by media opinion shapers seldom provide a full picture, one that can illuminate and help in spreading the "good news."

The essential aim here is to present our data—gleaned from polls, interviews, and other findings—in an objective way. We felt that how a representative group of people from all over the United States articulated their thoughts could be helpful. No specific theological statements are made for any particular denomination or creed. "To see him as Americans see him" was the aim, and this could be best determined by modern scientific methods of polling.

Statistics, of course, are only as valid as their interpretation. But even expert poll evaluators can become bogged down in numbers and comparisons as they try to discern trends and meanings. The interpretations offered here will lead the interested reader to the tables in the Appendix, which contain many of the polls' findings.

Some of the most informative and illuminating pictures of contemporary America have been provided by Studs Terkel, the nationally syndicated newspaper columnist, talk-show host, and gadfly of Chicago politics. For his "oral histories," he tape-records and edits interviews with a wide range of people: rich and poor, famous and little-known, powerful and powerless. The five books that have resulted so far provide many new insights and perceptions that add depth to attitude surveys and other data.

In chapters 2, 4, and 6 we have incorporated similar material. We call them "voices," and they are presented in the conviction that they can add perceptions and even provide some personal identification. We are especially grateful to the persons interviewed in chapter 6 for permission to quote their comments.

The greatest problem we found was keeping the focus on contemporary perceptions of Jesus. As the Gospel of John says (21:25), "There are many other things that Jesus did. If they were all written down one by one, I suppose that the whole world could not hold the books that would be written."

This book attempts to make an addition to the body of knowledge that has developed over some twenty centuries and—most important—to guide those who seek to understand their own beliefs in the light of contemporary American Christianity.

1

The Issues

Jesus went to the territory near the town of Caesarea
Philippi, where he asked his disciples, "Who do people
say the Son of Man is?"

"Some say John the Baptist," they answered. "Others
say Elijah, while others say Jeremiah or some other
prophet."

"What about you?" he asked them. "Who do you say I
am?"

Simon Peter answered, "You are the Messiah, the Son
of the living God."

—Matthew 16:13–16

We could say that Jesus was conducting an opinion poll when
he asked these questions. His disciples answered as truthfully as
they could. They had mingled with the multitudes that gathered
when Jesus preached. And even though they lacked the modern
scientific poll-taker's expertise, most would agree that their response was a fair evaluation of then-current sentiments.

Did Jesus' questions stem from a desire to know what people
were saying about him, or was he merely testing his followers?
In either case, Peter's answer was forthright and unequivocal.
Not all Jesus' disciples were as certain, and even Peter did not
grasp the implications of what he had said. When Jesus foretold
his coming suffering and death, Peter argued back, "That must
never happen to you!" (Matt. 16:22).

Even after Jesus' death and resurrection, Thomas was skeptical. "Unless I see the scars of the nails in his hands and put my
finger on those scars and my hand in his side, I will not believe"
(John 20:25). Thomas was present the next time Jesus appeared

to the disciples. Jesus asked Thomas to examine his hands and side and said, "Stop your doubting, and believe" (20:27b). Thomas gave a cry of recognition: "My Lord and my God!" (20:28). Then Jesus said, "Do you believe because you see me? How happy are those who believe without seeing me!" (20:29).

Thomas had direct "seeing-is-believing" evidence. But uncounted millions over the centuries have not seen but have still believed. Since Christ's resurrection there have been many Forthright Peters and Doubting Thomases. However, there can be little doubt that belief in Jesus and his message has significantly influenced—in one way or another—the history and culture of the modern world. As one anonymous writer has suggested:

> He was born in an obscure village,
>   the child of a peasant woman.
> He grew up in still another village
>   where he worked until he was thirty.
> Then for three years
>   he was an itinerant preacher.
> He never wrote a book.
> He never held an office.
> He never had a family or owned a home.
> He didn't go to college.
> He never traveled more than 200 miles
>   from the place he was born.
> He did none of the things
>   one usually associates with greatness.
> He had no credentials but himself;
>   he was only thirty-three
>   when public opinion turned against him.
> His friends ran away.
> He was turned over to his enemies
>   and went through the mockery of a trial.
> He was nailed to a cross
>   between two thieves.
> While he was dying
>   his executioners gambled for his clothing,
>   the only property he had on earth.
> When he was dead
>   he was laid in a borrowed grave
>   through the pity of a friend.

Nineteen centuries have come and gone
and today he is the central figure
of the human race,
the leader of mankind's progress.
All the armies that ever marched,
all the navies that ever sailed,
all the parliaments that ever sat,
all the kings that ever reigned,
put together,
have not affected
the life of man on earth
as much as that
One Solitary Life.

The New Testament Gospels tell of miracles that Jesus per-formed in healing the sick, quieting storms, and other wonders, but surely the greatest miracle, dwarfing all others, was inspiring his followers to spread his message throughout the world over the course of twenty centuries. Many men have proclaimed themselves the Messiah foretold in the Scriptures. None has achieved anything more than an ephemeral following.

The millions of dedicated Christians who came after Peter and the now-believing Thomas have had only the Gospels and the teachings of Jesus' followers, but they have been certain that Jesus has come into their lives.

Every age of every culture has had those who strive for some kind of meaning beyond just existing and surviving. There seems to be a profound universal need for humans to believe in some-thing outside themselves. Many have found it in Christ and his teachings. Their beliefs led some to piety, sacrifice, and martyr-dom, others to create great works of literature, art, architecture, and music that enriched the world.

But it should also be noted that many crimes and inhumane acts were committed in the name of Christianity. Some who profess the Christian faith have used it for their own selfish ends and have manipulated both Christians and non-Christians to achieve status, political power, and personal gain in ways that Christ would have deplored.

Until fairly recently, questions of what people think about Jesus have had to be approached in intuitive and haphazard ways. Modern scientific poll-taking began only in the 1930s, and relatively little opinion research was done in the field of religion until the 1960s. Even less concern was focused on the essence of Christianity—beliefs about Jesus Christ.

Within certain small margins of error, the new scientific opinion-sampling techniques that have developed over the past fifty years have proved reliable in assessing where specific groups stand on given issues. A representative sampling allows poll-takers to project attitudes and feelings of an entire group with considerable accuracy.

To be fully effective in determining attitudes, however, a well-conceived poll must go beyond mere head-counting. The depth of feeling, understanding, and commitment on a given issue is often more important than simple yes-or-no responses can indicate.

One of the caveats in interpreting poll data is that the results are valid only for the time period during which the questions were asked. Wide swings in approval or disapproval of political candidates, consumer products, and entertainment personalities can and do happen virtually overnight. But in matters of basic religious or philosophical values, attitudes and beliefs have tended to remain relatively stable, changing very slowly, if at all.

Recent polls, and other signs, however, indicate a rising tide of interest and involvement in religion among all levels of American society, but particularly among Protestants. For example, nearly 6 of 10 Americans say that they are more interested in religious and spiritual matters than they were just five years ago.

Some observers see this as the first crocus of spring: a sure sign of an awakening or even a sweeping religious revival. Others, less sanguine perhaps, point to other data, showing that while those polled may feel more concerned about religion, the respondees doubt that the public as a whole shares their feelings. However, virtually everyone feels that it is important to stress spiritual and ethical values.

Christianity is the predominant religious affiliation professed by Americans; our culture and even our laws reflect it. However, Christianity is a big umbrella that covers a wide variety of attitudes and commitments. But Jesus and his teachings are at the core of Christianity, and American perceptions of him (his image, if you will) are worthy of careful study.

That is the principal thrust of this book: to present pertinent data, provide some historical perspectives and insights, assess the impact on individuals, churches, and society, and venture some thoughts about the lessons that can be learned.

2

Perceptions

Jesus took the blind man by the hand and led him out of
the village. After spitting on the man's eyes, Jesus placed
his hands on him and asked him, "Can you see
anything?"
The man looked up and said, "Yes, I can see people,
but they look like trees walking around."
Jesus again placed his hands on the man's eyes. This
time the man looked intently, his eyesight returned, and
he saw everything clearly.
—Mark 8:23–25

American adults overwhelmingly consider themselves Christians. In round figures, the 166 million American civilians eigh-
teen years of age or older include 81 percent who so classify
themselves. Of these 166 million, 20 percent consider themselves to be evangelicals; 80 percent do not.

But within that overwhelming percentage of Christians, we
must consider that there are "devout" Christians and "nominal"
Christians. There are "practicing" Christians and "lip-service"
Christians, and many gradations in between. Mother Teresa, for
instance, ministering to the poor and afflicted in Calcutta, and an
inner-city dope peddler both might classify themselves as Christians, but obviously their degree of commitment to Christian
principles is vastly different. And within the general term "Christian" there are also many cultural, ethnic, age, and other varia-
tions.

Any study of consequence would properly begin with Americans' ideas about Jesus. He is, after all, the core of the Christian
faith. If that core is not solid, all else drops away into insignifi-

cance. But despite the large majority reporting themselves as Christians, a significant proportion do not subscribe to some basic Christian doctrines. And a shockingly high percentage seem ignorant of some fundamental biblical facts.

Beliefs, attitudes, and actions are usually shaped by perceptions—how each of us learns or is taught to view persons and events. What then are American perceptions of Jesus Christ?

Research indicates that our image of Christ—while a bit murky in spots—is overwhelmingly favorable. Moreover, there are fewer differences in perceptions based on such factors as age, sex, and educational level than might be expected. The key attributes that American Christians spontaneously ascribe to Jesus are selfless love, compassion, kindness, and capacity to forgive.

The perceptions that led to these attitudes logically start with the most basic question:

Do you believe that Jesus Christ ever actually lived?

The intent of the question was to separate those who doubt or deny the existence of Jesus on earth from those who acknowledge—at the very least—that he lived, in a historical sense. Some 91 percent (about 145 million adult Americans) believe that he did live, that there was indeed a person called Jesus living in Israel in the period in which the Romans dominated the area. (See Table 1, in Appendix.)

When a corollary question was asked of those who believed that he had lived—**Do you think he was God, or just another religious leader like Mohammed or Buddha?**—the affirmative percentage shrank somewhat. Overall, 70 percent felt that he was indeed God. Another 11 percent felt that he was just "another religious leader," while another 10 percent answered "other" or "don't know." A scant 2 percent of the public at large replied, "No, Christ did not live," and the remaining 7 percent said, "Don't know." (See Table 1.)

Perhaps the most interesting finding from this particular group of questions concerned respondents who believed that Jesus lived but not that he was God. Asked **Do you wish you could believe in the divinity of Jesus,** a surprisingly high 20 percent answered yes. Some 44 percent felt it didn't make much difference, and 36 percent said they didn't know. (See Table 2.)

We can conjecture that many felt there was a vacuum in their own lives which they saw filled in the lives of their believing Christian friends and neighbors.

The pivotal question and the one that provides the ultimate perception concerns the deity of Christ. If he was indeed God incarnate—and this is the orthodox Christian view—there could be no reason to doubt or question his teachings, except perhaps through misunderstanding or misinterpreting them.

The way a question is asked sometimes can make a significant difference. In one poll Americans were asked:

Which ONE of these statements comes closest to describing your beliefs about Jesus?

Only 42 percent of the public at large chose the statement "Jesus was divine in the sense that he was in fact God living among men." Even those who said that religion was very important to them registered only a slim majority (52 percent). Some 27 percent chose the option "Jesus was divine in the sense that while he was only a man, he was uniquely called by God to reveal God's purpose in the world." Alternative possible responses were: "Jesus was divine in the sense that he embodied the best that is in all men" (9 percent) and "Jesus was a great man and teacher, but I could not call him divine" (6 percent). Others doubted that Jesus ever existed (2 percent) or had no opinion (14 percent). (See Table 3.)

But when the question was phrased another way in a different poll, the results were quite different. Americans were asked:

In your own life, how important is the belief that Christ was fully God and fully human?

Eighty-one percent of the public at large reported that this belief was either "very important" (58 percent) or "fairly important" (23 percent). Protestants (67 percent) were more likely than Catholics (58 percent) to report "very important," while Catholics (29 percent) were more likely to view it as "fairly important."

Gender also seemed to be a factor. More women (66 percent) felt that this belief was "very important" as against only 50 percent of the men, and a significant 12 percent of the men reported that it was "not very important." Southern Baptists (81 percent) led in "very important" responses.

Age also figured significantly in the responses. Among the

18-to-29 group, 53 percent reported "very important"; whereas among the 50-and-older group, 66 percent agreed with the "fully God and fully human" concept.

The widest disparity occurred between those who classified themselves as "evangelicals" and those who said they were "non-evangelicals." This belief was "very important" to evangelicals (92 percent); among non-evangelicals the figure was only 49 percent.

The "not very important," "not at all important," and "no opinion" responses were distinct minorities, although for those who grouped themselves among liberals in religious ideology, about one third considered the belief "not very important" or "not at all important." (See Table 4.)

In the New Testament (Matt. 26:64; John 14:3), Jesus promised to reappear on earth, a belief usually referred to as the Second Coming. Do Americans accept this as literally true or question it? Americans were asked:

According to the Bible, Jesus promised to return to earth someday. Do you have serious doubts that this will happen, have some doubts that this will happen, or have no doubts that this will happen?

The results showed that among those with strong religious convictions the belief in the Second Coming is held by an overwhelming proportion (almost 80 percent) in all groups. But, more surprisingly perhaps, a representative sample of *all* Americans showed that more than 6 in 10 (62 percent) harbored "no doubts" about a Second Coming. Among the public at large, only 1 in 4 have either "some doubts" (16 percent) or "serious doubts" (10 percent). And a small percentage (1 percent) *volunteered* the view that the Second Coming had already taken place or is happening now. Although not statistically significant, it is interesting to note that 4 percent of those who are "making the greatest effort to follow Jesus' example" spontaneously ventured this opinion. (See Table 5.)

We have seen that Americans perceive Christ in a highly favorable light, whether they believe that he was God or man or both.

But why? Why does a first-century Jewish carpenter and

teacher exert such tremendous influence on our lives today? What personal characteristics or traits explain his appeal? What universal chord did he strike, and what deeply felt human needs did his message contain?

There are no descriptions of Jesus' physical appearance in the Bible. What did he look like? Was he tall or short, slim or portly? What color were his eyes and his hair and how was it cut? Was his preaching style florid or restrained? In today's electronic age it is a given that one's personality, appearance, and manner are keys to public acceptance, but since contemporary descriptions of Jesus are sketchy or nonexistent, we can only picture his personal and physical characteristics from what he said and the reactions of his followers.

Great artists have given us their interpretations of how Jesus the man may have appeared, based on some knowledge of the customs of his time and the Middle East (more about this in chapter 3). Our perceptions of him are undoubtedly influenced by their work.

A representative cross section of Americans were asked:

What do you consider to be the most appealing character or personality traits of Jesus?

Some twenty were spontaneously mentioned. Forty-one percent mentioned his "love for humankind," a response that led all others by a 3-to-1 margin. Thirteen percent mentioned "forgiveness," 9 percent "kindness," 7 percent "compassion" and "help and guidance." "Humility," "knowledge and understanding," "caring," "teachings," "promise of salvation," and "everything about him is good" were mentioned by 6 percent of the respondents.

Americans with strong religious convictions tended to mention each trait as frequently or more frequently as those in the sample as a whole. The "promise of salvation" that Jesus extended is also noted by 11 percent of those making the greatest possible effort to follow Jesus' example. (See Table 6.)

A more complex question asked respondents to describe Jesus. They were shown cards listing contrasting pairs of words describing personality traits and presented with a scale of 1 to 7. Arithmetic means were calculated on the basis of responses. The smaller (closer to 1) or the larger (closer to 7) the resulting mean, the closer to these extremes that people pictured Jesus.

For instance, Americans generally felt that Jesus was more "warm" (1 on the scale) than "aloof" (7 on the scale); the mean score on this question was 1.5.

The other mean scores show that Americans are overwhelmingly of the opinion that Jesus was brave (not cowardly), emotionally stable (not unstable), had a strong (not weak) personality, was without sin (not sinful), and perfect (not imperfect). Americans also tend toward the view—but by less impressive margins—that Jesus was easy (rather than hard) to understand, physically strong (rather than weak), practical (rather than impractical), physically attractive (rather than unattractive), divine (rather than human), and accepting (rather than demanding). The public at large was divided on whether Jesus was fun-loving or somber. (See Table 7.)

Statistical data like the foregoing can be useful tools, but they are essentially sterile. They provide a framework but not a full understanding of the overall picture. Humans approach the eternal mystery of God in many ways, usually intuitively, sometimes intellectually, and often both. But Americans often become inarticulate when trying to express their deepest feelings or to put their finger on the precise reasons they feel as they do. And when the subject deals with God, their own mortality, and the meaning of their lives, this difficulty is even more pronounced. Experienced poll-takers recognize this, of course, and usually try to devise surveys to suggest a range of options that might reveal the truest feelings.

While polls can accurately reflect "who" believes "what" about Jesus, they are less effective in getting at the "why." The reasons are as individual as fingerprints, but they can also be revealing. Not everyone can put these perceptions into words. A forty-four-year-old Palmdale, California, woman, for instance, replied, to a pollster's question, "I don't always understand the why of him; I just know he helps."

The authors conducted follow-up and in-depth interviews with a randomly selected but representative sample of Americans who could express their perceptions more effectively. It was hoped that their views would illuminate what others think—as well as what they believed themselves. Among the results:

A thirty-seven-year-old well-spoken Montana farmer who now considers himself a "born-again Christian" told us, "I see in Jesus all the qualities that I have come to admire. I was born and raised as a Christian, but mostly I just went through the motions. . . . Church on Sunday if the fish weren't biting, for instance. Then one Sunday about Eastertime I watched a TV show, 'Jesus of Nazareth.' As I watched I felt the hairs on the back of my neck standing up and a kind of tingling along my spine. He [the actor] portrayed my conception of Jesus perfectly. He was just saying a lot of the things I'd heard in church and Sunday school, but the feeling was so intense . . . so vivid . . . that I cried.

"Maybe it was just a latent feeling, something that carried over, but I was moved. Really moved. I began to study the Bible and listen more closely in church. I feel much better about myself today and I think—I can hope, anyway—that I am closer to following him."

A fifty-seven-year-old nurse's aide, a black woman from a New York suburb, said simply, "I just know that he is my Savior. I pray and he answers."

A forty-eight-year-old lawyer from Washington State explained, "Once you accept that there is indeed a Supreme Being, you have to look for some evidence that Jesus lived. There is abundant evidence. Once you accept the fact that he lived and was the Son of God, you have to heed his teachings. My wife is a Christian, and she got me started in studying the subject. Once I accepted God and Jesus, the rest was easy. I immediately felt *simpatico* with all that he preached—love of one another, compassion, hope, etc. I sometimes disagree with my church's leaders, but there is always that image of Christ in my mind."

A sixty-eight-year-old philosophy professor from New England had a warning. "What you're doing [surveying Americans' perceptions of Jesus] is 'subjectivism.' You're only quantifying what people think, not necessarily what is historically true and relevant about Jesus and his teachings. I happen to admire many of the things recounted in the Gospels, but I can't help questioning their authenticity. The Gospel writers were, after all, writing many years later—after the fact. I'd feel more comfortable if some Pulitzer Prize journalists or historians had been on hand. Maybe then there would be less confusion about who he was, what he was like, what he said, and maybe even what he meant."

Said a twenty-two-year-old mechanic, "What are my impressions of Jesus? I often think of him as a smart older brother. I think of God the Father as stern but rather aloof. Loving, sure, but demanding too. Something like my own dad, I guess. Jesus is more like an older brother, who understands me and forgives me when I stray a bit. But he also encourages me and helps me to do the right thing. I never had a brother, but I sometimes wish I had. Does that sound crazy?"

A thirty-three-year-old Maine educator, an active Vietnam War protester and feminist, said that to her Jesus represents "compassion and forgiveness." She goes to church infrequently, mostly she says because she is turned off by the hellfire-and-damnation approach of some clergy.

A seventy-four-year-old retiree, a native of Ohio who has been active in charities and public service activities, said that he had trouble with the "divinity" concept. "I agree that he was an inspiring teacher, and I try to live by his teachings—especially the Sermon on the Mount. But I've never been able to really make the commitment to the God-man idea. About his divinity, I don't know. I don't think we can really *know.*"

Asked her perceptions of Jesus, a thirty-one-year-old psychiatric nurse at a New York hospital answered facetiously at first. "Which one? We've got three on our unit." She went on—"I'm sorry, I couldn't resist my little joke"—to explain that "a common delusion among our really sick patients is that they are God or Jesus or Napoleon or Alexander the Great or even the reincarnation of Elvis Presley. I haven't kept score, but I'd guess that the Jesus delusion is the most common. I don't mean that to sound hard or cynical, although it's easy to get that way in psych nursing. Many of us are in the so-called 'caring professions' because we *really do care.* Jesus was compassionate. To me that's his most appealing characteristic. We see a few miracle cures here, but most of the time we can only hope for improvement, enough anyway so that the patient can reenter society and be effective. There's always hope. That's what Jesus taught and that's what keeps us going."

And, finally a self-proclaimed atheist quoted a line from a movie he had seen: "To you [a Christian] I'm the enemy; to Jesus I'm the loyal opposition."

3

Jesus as Viewed Through the Ages

Now, there are many other things that Jesus did. If they were all written down one by one, I suppose that the whole world could not hold the books that would be written.

John 21:25

John's vision of a world flooded by books about Jesus can be considered a bit of hyperbole. It hasn't happened. Not yet, anyway, even though it sometimes seems that way and this book may add to the inundation.

The output of material about Jesus is indeed immense, not only in books but also in art, music, drama, and dance. Each in its own way has affected many of our perceptions of him. Christians have come through these twenty centuries to today's perceptions over a difficult and challenging course. The way Christians think of Jesus and his teachings has changed and evolved with each generation. These changes have often reflected the political, social, and philosophical problems of a given era. Some would say they have also been *part* of the problems.

We are here concerned primarily with today's Americans' perceptions of Jesus. To attempt to detail the currents and cross-currents of twenty centuries of history is beyond the mission and the competence of the authors. Nonetheless, as Shakespeare said, "What's past is prologue," so some review—even a superficial one—will help give some kind of perspective on how Jesus is perceived.

Our perceptions come to us from the New Testament: principally the Gospels of Matthew, Mark, Luke, and John and the various epistles. In addition, we have inferences drawn from fragmented knowledge of the spiritual and political climate of his time and the places where he lived.

Jesus himself wrote nothing that we know of. The Gospels—whether or not one considers them divinely inspired—were written more as evangelistic tracts than as biography or history. Almost everyone, however, would acknowledge that they are majestic in language and inspiring in tone. They portray the quintessential Jesus and his message to humankind, but they leave unanswered many questions about what kind of person he was.

Modern biographers and historians contend that nothing about a great person is unimportant. They search for the tiniest shred of evidence about the subject's actions and philosophy. What did he or she say (or fail to say), do (or not do), and what could have been the reasons why (or why not)? Persons of the most profound faith in Jesus have asked such questions.

By anyone's definition Jesus qualifies as a great man, so the search to see him more clearly and understand his message has occupied many great and not-so-great minds of history. They have added to our understanding and sometimes possible misunderstandings of him.

One philosophical historian interviewed put it this way:

"Think of the efforts to understand Jesus as a jigsaw puzzle. An experienced puzzle fan looks for the four corner pieces first. The New Testament Gospels are the four corners of the Jesus puzzle, the parameters. Next the puzzler looks for the pieces with straight edges that form the borders. We can consider them, in this analogy, somewhat like the other records of Jesus' time, the usual raw materials of historians.

"Filling in the center portions with the puzzle clues offered by colors, shapes, and recognizable objects becomes the real test. The puzzle-solver experiments, tries this piece or that piece to see if it fits and harmonizes with the complete picture.

"We are still searching for some of those missing pieces from the center of the puzzle."

Theology and philosophy have made great strides over the years in understanding Jesus and his message, but their findings can't be as reproducible and conclusive as, say, a moon landing. We are still faced with the eternal mystery of God and Jesus. Jesus taught in broad principles. His audiences were common people, the farmers, laborers, fishermen, and artisans of Galilee and Judea. His parables, stories that his listeners could understand and identify with, illustrated the principles he wanted to inculcate.

Later it became evident to many through his teachings, personal magnetism, and miracles that he was indeed the Messiah promised in the Scriptures. The Scriptures, however, seemed to indicate to many of his followers that the promised Messiah would be an earthly king, one who would free them of oppressive foreign rule. Despite Jesus' denials of earthly ambitions ("My kingdom is not of this world"), these misperceptions persisted, even up to his death. But the triumph of his resurrection rallied his followers, set in motion the worldwide movement that is today's Christianity, and created many of the perceptions we have of him.

At this point a fast-forward on history's time machine can take us from Christ's time to the beginnings of the American experience. We will look briefly at the major influences that Christianity has had on Americans from the time of the first European settlers and then try to trace how their perceptions of Jesus influenced them and the course of American history. Later on we will look back at some of the origins of today's attitudes and suggest how they came to be.

Americans inherited many perceptions of Jesus from Europeans. Dissent from established religious practices was a principal impetus for the earliest emigrations from Europe to establish permanent settlements in the New World. But these new colonists differed from one another in their many interpretations of Christianity as much as they differed from the established religions in their homelands. The Puritans of the Massachusetts Bay Colony, for instance, saw Jesus in a different light from that of the Quakers of William Penn's colony in Pennsylvania or the Catholics in the Maryland colony led by Lord Baltimore.

The various colonies were relatively isolated by geography, and, although there were frictions, the colonists more and more insisted that the freedom to worship as one chose was an inherent right. With the coming of the Revolutionary War, religious differences were set aside and the colonists united to oppose the British. Once independence was won, the Founding Fathers deemed it both wise and expedient to include in the Constitution's Bill of Rights provisions that barred any state-sponsored religion and allowed citizens to worship—or not worship—as they might choose.

When the first federal census was taken in 1790, the three most numerous Christian groups in the thirteen original colonies were the products of the British colonial experience: Congregationalists, Presbyterians, and Episcopalians. They stemmed from the English Reformation and its Puritan aftermath. However, the 1790 census indicated that only about 5 percent of the populace identified with a specific church.

The First Amendment prohibition of the establishment of religion came about because rationalists such as Thomas Jefferson and James Madison and evangelical Christians shared a common goal. The latter, however, viewed the separation of church and state less as a way of cutting churches off from influencing secular affairs than as a way of preventing the state from telling anyone how to worship. Thus the second clause in the amendment forbids Congress to prohibit the free exercise of religion.

In Europe anticlericalism had been a factor in the revolutions of the late eighteenth and early nineteenth centuries. The Christians in the New World who worked successfully to disestablish those state religions that remained (Congregational in Massachusetts and Connecticut, for instance) found support from Baptists, Quakers, Presbyterians, and Roman Catholics. The principle of religious pluralism served the nation well over its first two centuries of independence. In effect, it created a "hands-off" atmosphere and a kind of religious laissez-faire that allowed religion and religious commitment to flourish.

Succeeding waves of immigrants brought many other religious traditions and national cultures, and while religious prejudices and sectarian animosities, along with racism and xenophobia, have persisted in American history, the courts and Congress have defended the constitutional concepts of pluralism and separation of church and state.

The concept of church-state separation remains a basic tenet of Americans' beliefs through the mid-1980s, but questions about prayers in school, abortion, and involvement in political and economic issues have become controversial issues. Contemporary polls clearly indicate that, among Americans who were aware of the issues, most had no objections to the clergy's speaking out in general terms on the religious dimensions of public policies (Table 8), but they did object to their direct involvement in the political process.

By a 5-to-3 ratio, Americans felt that it was wrong for religious groups to work actively for the defeat of political candidates who don't agree with their positions on issues. (See Table 9.) By a smaller ratio, Americans felt that religious organizations should not try to persuade senators and representatives to enact legislation that they would like to see become law. (See Table 10.)

Further evidence can be deduced from the findings of another survey, in which over half of the respondents said that it is wrong for political candidates to bring in their own political beliefs in discussing issues facing the nation. And by an even greater margin, they expressed the belief that it is wrong for members of the clergy to cite their own political beliefs in their sermons.

A major result of pluralism and increasing emigration to America was rampant sectarianism. Differences in theology and biblical interpretation—often minor—as well as ethnic and nationalistic traditions spawned a great variety of new denominations. And the movement to new frontiers in the West from the established eastern-seaboard colonies created new attitudes and problems.

By 1850, just sixty years after the first federal census, the first dominant eastern Protestant denominations—Congregationalists, Presbyterians, and Episcopalians—had been replaced as the most populous religious communities by Baptists, Methodists, and Roman Catholics.

Today, some 135 years later, about 20 percent of the nation's adults claim various Baptist churches as their religious preference, while Methodist churches claim some 9 percent. (See Table 11.) Catholic churches, meanwhile, could note the allegiance of some 28 percent of the total population. (See Table 12.)

Preaching by priests and ministers, powerful church art, sacred music, and awe-inspiring rituals all influenced perceptions of Jesus profoundly through the Middle Ages. The Reformation, the Renaissance, and the coincident development of movable type added a new dimension. The printed word became the most effective means of communication. Virtually everyone could now have access to a Bible; books, pamphlets, and religious tracts proliferated. Combined with increasing literacy, the availability of the printed word provided ready reference to believers in need of guidance or solace. Probably the most significant aspect of the printed word on perceptions of Jesus, however, was that —as one witty modern scholar put it—"He got a good press."

Theologians, philosophers, historians, essayists, novelists, and other shapers of thought may have differed widely on religion's role in human development, but virtually all have had only praise for Jesus the person and his message. Leaders in almost every occupation invariably have detractors, iconoclastic snipers who delight in questioning and demolishing beliefs, whatever they might be. Jesus has had few serious ones. He has indeed had a good press over the ages, and his teachings and his example have struck a universal chord.

Chapter 6 presents some contemporary American perceptions of Jesus to supplement the data gathered from various polls and to add a revealing dimension to the statistics.

We have no scientific poll data from before the mid-1930s, but many voices have been raised and preserved in writing. Jesus was such a compelling figure that believers and nonbelievers, saints and sinners, agnostics and atheists, clerics and anticlerics, and even leaders in other religions, such as Islam, Hinduism, and Buddhism, acknowledged the positive influence of his teachings.

These voices from the past—while not representative in a poll-taking sense—in many ways shaped how the world perceives Jesus.

For instance, even those who have rejected the idea of God or a First Cause, much less the concept of Jesus as both God and man, applaud the essential Jesus. An American writer, lawyer, and lecturer of the late nineteenth century, Robert Ingersoll, created a great stir by publicly questioning the existence of God and lambasting Christian doctrines and churchmen. Yet he could write:

> For the man Christ who loved his fellow men and believed in
> the Infinite Father, who would shield the innocent and protect the

just; for the martyr who expected to be rescued from the cruel cross, and who at last, finding that his hope was dust, cried out in the gathering gloom, "My God, my God, why hast thou forsaken me?"—for that great and suffering man I have the highest admiration and respect. They crucified a kind and perfectly innocent man. Had I lived in his day I would have been his friend. His life is worth its example—its moral force, its heroism of benevolence. For that name I have infinite respect and love. To that great and serene man I gladly pay my homage of admiration and my tears. (Quoted by Manuel Komroff in *Jesus Through the Centuries*, p. 491; William Sloane Associates, 1953)

Another non-Christian, the Indian political leader and Hindu ascetic Mohandas Gandhi, credited Jesus with being the inspiration for the passive resistance movement that led to his nation's independence. He quoted certain sayings of Jesus: "But I say unto you, That ye resist not evil" (Matt. 5:39, KJV) and "Love your enemies . . . pray for them which despitefully use you . . . that you may be the children of your Father which is in heaven" (Matt. 5:44–45, KJV).

For absolute unbelievers, John Stuart Mill, the nineteenth-century English philosopher, economist, rationalist, and developer of "utilitarianism," had these words:

And whatever else may be taken away from us by rational criticism, Christ is still left—a unique figure, not more unlike all his precursors than all his followers. . . .

About the life and sayings of Jesus there is a stamp of personal originality combined with profound insight; which, if we abandon the idle expectation of finding scientific precision where something very different was aimed at, must place the prophet of Nazareth, even in the estimation of those who have no belief in his inspiration, in the very first rank of the men of sublime genius of whom our species can boast. When this pre-eminent genius is combined with the qualities of probably the greatest moral reformer and martyr to that mission who ever existed upon earth, religion cannot be said to have made a bad choice in pitching on this man as the ideal representative and guide of humanity; nor even now would it be easy, even for an unbeliever, to find a better translation of the rule of virtue from the abstract into the concrete, than to endeavor so to live that Christ would approve our life. (Quoted by Manuel Komroff in *Jesus Through the Centuries*, p. 406)

A different voice is heard in Jean-Jacques Rousseau, the French philosopher and author whose writings frequently offended church and civil authorities in eighteenth-century France. He took umbrage at some of his contemporaries' attempts to equate the martyrdom of Jesus with that of the Greek philosopher Socrates. To be sure, there were some superficial similarities. Both were teachers of morals and ethics; neither had written anything that survived, but both were chronicled by their followers; both were tried and sentenced to death by local courts for the equivalent of sedition and the corrupting of established ways. But Rousseau could say, in his *Confessions:*

> What prepossession, what blindness, must it be to compare the son of Sophroniscus to the son of Mary! . . . [Socrates] invented, it is said, the theory of morals. Others, however, had before put them in practice; he had only to say, therefore, what they had done, and reduce their examples to precept. But where could Jesus learn, among his competitors, that pure and sublime morality of which he only has given us both precept and example? The death of Socrates, peacefully philosophizing with his friends, appears the most agreeable that could be wished for; that of Jesus, expiring in the midst of agonizing pain, abused, insulted, and accused by a whole nation, is the most horrible that could be feared. Socrates, in receiving the cup of poison, blessed the weeping executioner who administered it; but Jesus, in the midst of excruciating tortures, prayed for his merciless tormentors. Yes! if the life and death of Socrates were those of a sage, the life and death of Jesus were those of a God. Shall we suppose the evangelic history a mere fiction? Indeed, my friend, it bears not the marks of fiction; on the contrary, the history of Socrates, which nobody presumes to doubt, is not so well attested as that of Jesus Christ. . . . It is more inconceivable that a number of persons should agree to write such a history, than that one only should furnish the subject of it.

By the nineteenth century—a period of rationalism (some would say rationalizing)—questioning the scriptural accounts of Jesus' life on earth had become widespread. But, as the German philosopher Friedrich Nietzsche (who popularized the theory of the "superman," or natural aristocrat) could say, "If a man has strong faith, he can indulge in the luxury of skepticism."

And by then what had been the jealously guarded province of

theologians and philosophers had become of interest to many objective and empirical historians. Using the tools of the historian's trade, the weaving together of established facts and conjectures, they began to sift through the evidence. Did a man called Jesus ever actually live? Did he really claim to be divine? Was he indeed the Messiah promised in the Old Testament?

The French historian and philologist of the Hebrew language Ernest Renan is one nineteenth-century writer who investigated the roots of Christianity in a balanced and objective fashion. His book *The Life of Jesus,* published in 1863, was a bombshell. Widely praised and widely criticized, it came to be considered a starting point for further intense studies. Renan had stepped on many an ecclesiastical toe along the way and was attacked and villified by detractors, but he and those he inspired to follow his lead all added some new dimensions to our perceptions of Jesus.

Renan reaffirmed the existence of Jesus and pointed out the reasons why Christ could arouse the devotion of his followers:

> The essential work of Jesus was to create around him a circle of disciples, whom he inspired with boundless affection, and amongst whom he deposited the germ of his doctrine. To have made himself beloved, "to the degree that after his death they ceased not to love him," was the great work of Jesus, and that which most struck his contemporaries. His doctrine was so little dogmatic, that he never thought of writing it or causing it to be written. Men did not become his disciples by believing this thing or that thing, but in being attached to his person and in loving him. A few sentences collected from memory, and especially the type of character he set forth, and the impression it had left, were what remained of him. Jesus was not a founder of dogmas, or a maker of creeds; he infused into the world a new spirit. The least Christian men were, on the one hand, the doctors of the Greek Church, who, beginning from the fourth century, entangled Christianity in a path of puerile metaphysical discussions, and, on the other, the scholastics of the Latin Middle Ages, who wished to draw from the Gospel the thousands of articles of a colossal system. To follow Jesus in expectation of the kingdom of God, was all that first was implied by being Christian. . . .
>
> His perfect idealism is the highest rule of the unblemished and virtuous life. . . . The foundation of true religion is indeed his work; after him, all that remains is to develop it and render it fruitful.

Renan had made the search for the historic Jesus a respectable occupation. It cost him dearly in some respects, but he filled in some of the pieces in the jigsaw puzzle of Christ's life on earth.

He was followed by another Frenchman, Alfred Loisy (1857–1940), who devoted most of his career to studying the life of Jesus. He delved even more deeply into the historical records of Jesus' time and published some forty volumes of his studies. He wrote, in *The Birth of the Christian Religion:*

> Whatever may have been said to the contrary, there is not a single Christian document of the first age which does not imply the historicity of Jesus. The gnostic Docetists who denied the materiality of Christ's body and the physical reality of his Passion believed, with the mass of Christians, in the historicity of Jesus and of his appearance as a figure upon the earth; their Christ, immaterial but visible, was not for them an unreal phantom, a pure image of the mind, as our mythologues would sometimes make him out to have been. And pagan writers least favorable to the Christian religion, from Tacitus to Celsus and the Emperor Julian, always regarded Jesus as a historical figure, Christ being for them the name of a Galilean agitator who came to an evil end and whom his followers had absurdly made into a god.

Albert Schweitzer, one of the most compelling figures of our times, also took up the search. He was a Protestant theologian, an authority on church music and the composer Johann Sebastian Bach, and a medical missionary to equatorial Africa. In 1906 he published *The Quest of the Historical Jesus,* in which he concluded that the *historical* Jesus would continue to be an enigma.

> But the truth is, it is not Jesus as historically known, but Jesus as spiritually arisen within men, who is significant for our time and can help it. Not the historical Jesus, but the spirit which goes forth from Him. . . . The abiding and eternal in Jesus is absolutely independent of historical knowledge and can only be understood by contact with His spirit which is still at work in the world. In proportion as we have the Spirit of Jesus we have the true knowledge of Jesus.

As the founder of a hospital in the African jungle, Dr. Schweitzer went on to practice what Jesus preached.

Historians can infer from records and other data the effects that a given human figure might have had on human history. But Jesus has been accorded another dimension, a divine one as the Son of God. To see Jesus in this context required more than historical research. It needed what has become known as "the leap of faith."

"It is the heart that senses God, not reason." So said Blaise Pascal, a seventeenth-century Frenchman and one of the most brilliant minds of his or any other age. As a child prodigy, he made many contributions to theoretical and applied mathematics. He developed a mechanical calculating machine that was a forerunner of today's computers. He also was a father of probability theory, the basis of much of what we know about projecting statistics such as the ones that are an integral part of this book.

Despite his background in rigid mathematical and physical disciplines, or perhaps because of it, Pascal came to believe that there are limits to the human intellect. His own turning point from mathematical prodigy to mystical contemplation and writing seemed to come when he narrowly escaped death in a carriage accident and came to believe that his survival was a miracle. He was thirty-one years old.

Was he a "near-death survivor," like those to be described in the next chapter, people who may have had a glimpse into a hereafter after nearly dying? At any rate, he spent most of the rest of his life in an earnest search for God and an understanding of Jesus.

His *Pensées (Thoughts),* a collection of fragmented notes and writings published after his death, indicate some of his perceptions of Jesus. He wrote:

> Great geniuses have their power, their glory, their greatness, their victory, their lustre, and have no need of worldly greatness, with which they are not in keeping. They are seen, not by the eye, but by the mind; this is sufficient. . . .
>
> Jesus Christ, without riches, and without any external exhibition of knowledge, is in His own order of holiness. He did not invent, He did not reign. But He was humble, patient, holy, holy to God, terrible to devils, without any sin. Oh! in what great pomp, and in what wonderful splendour, He is come to the eyes of the heart, which perceive wisdom!

Pascal also noted a characteristic of Jesus that anyone trying to communicate thoughts—Christian ministers, preachers, artists, writers, whoever—should heed.

> Jesus Christ said great things so simply, that it seems as though He had not thought them great; and yet so clearly that we easily see what He thought of them. This clearness, joined to this simplicity, is wonderful.

Despite his championing of simplicity and clarity, Pascal was probably less effective and eloquent for our time than the migrant Okie preacher in the classic twentieth-century American novel by John Steinbeck, *The Grapes of Wrath*. Steinbeck has his preacher say:

> "I ain't saying I'm like Jesus. But I got tired like Him, an' I got mixed up like Him, an' I went into the wilderness like Him, without no campin' stuff. Nighttime I'd lay on my back an' look up at the stars; morning I'd set an' watch the sun come up. . . .
> "An' I got to thinkin', on'y it wasn't thinkin', it was deeper down than thinkin'. I got thinkin' how we was holy when we was one thing, an' mankin' was holy when it was one thing. . . . But when they're all workin' together, not one fella for another fella, but one fella kind of harnessed to the whole shebang—that's right, that's holy."

Americans think of Russia as an atheistic nation, and officially it certainly is. The state is god, and Marx and Lenin are its prophets. But Christianity persists there despite harassment, repression, and official disapproval. Perhaps this is because Christianity seems to thrive when persecuted. More likely, though, it reflects some aspects of the Russian psyche and the perceptions of Jesus described by those giants of Russian literature, the nineteenth-century writers Turgenev, Tolstoy, and Dostoevski.

Ivan Turgenev, for instance, a champion of the lowly and oppressed, told in his *Poems in Prose* of a youthful encounter with someone whom he perceived to be Jesus. He recounted that he was in a village church, surrounded by brown-haired Russian peasants, when

> suddenly some one stepped in behind me, and placed himself near me.

I did not turn, but had nevertheless a feeling that this man—was Christ.

I was overcome by emotion, curiosity, and fright all at once. I controlled myself, and looked at my neighbors.

He had a countenance like other people's—a countenance like any other man's face. The eyes were looking softly and attentively upward. The lips were closed, but not compressed; the upper lip seemed to rest on the lower. His beard was not long and was parted at the chin. His hands were folded and motionless. Even his dress was like that of others.

Can this be Christ? I thought—such an unpretending, perfectly simple person? It is not possible.

I turned away, but scarcely had I withdrawn my glance from this plain man when it seemed to me that he who was standing by me must really be Christ.

I looked at him once more, and again I saw the same face that looked like the faces of all other men; the same every-day though unfamiliar features.

At last I became uncomfortable, and collected myself. Then it suddenly became clear to me that Christ had really just such a common human face.

Turgenev's youthful experience—seeing Christ in everyone—undoubtedly influenced his later decision to free the serfs on the estates he inherited and to write extensively about social conditions in Russia.

A Turgenev contemporary, Leo Tolstoy, author of those classic novels *War and Peace* and *Anna Karenina,* among many others, came to his clear perceptions of Jesus at an older age. He wrote:

For thirty-five years of my life, I was, in the proper acceptance of the word, a nihilist—not a revolutionary socialist, but a man who believed nothing. Five years ago my faith came to me. I believed in the doctrines of Jesus, and my whole life underwent a sudden transformation. . . . Life and death ceased to be evil; instead of despair I tasted joy and happiness that death could not take away. (Quoted by Manuel Komroff in *Jesus Through the Centuries,* p. 375)

The experience could be considered a classic example of the "born-again Christian" experience.

In "My Religion," an essay about his faith, Tolstoy explained:

> I believe that nothing but the fulfillment of the doctrine of Jesus can give true happiness to men. I believe that the fulfillment of this doctrine is possible, easy, and pleasant. I believe that although none other follows this doctrine, and I alone am left to practice it, I cannot refuse to obey it, if I would save my life from the certainty of eternal loss; just as a man in a burning house if he find a door to safety, must go out, so must I avail myself of the way to salvation. I believe that my life according to the doctrine of the world has been a torment, and that a life according to the doctrine of Jesus can alone give me in this world the happiness for which I was destined by the Father of Life. I believe that this doctrine is essential to the welfare of humanity, will save me from the certainty of eternal loss, and will give me in this world the greatest possible sum of happiness. Believing thus, I am obliged to practice its commandments. . . .

> Jesus has demonstrated that fellowship with the son of man, the love of men for one another, is not merely an ideal after which men are to strive; he has shown us that this love and this fellowship are natural attributes of men in their normal condition, the condition into which children are born, the condition in which all men would live if they were not drawn aside by error, illusions, and temptations.

4

Jesus' Influence
on Americans Today

"But anyone who hears these words of mine and does not obey them is like a foolish man who built his house on sand."
                                                        —Matthew 7:26

How Americans perceive Jesus is important, of course, but how do their views affect their daily lives? In what ways does Jesus enter their lives, and how closely do they follow his precepts and example? How have these perceptions influenced not only their lives but also the institutions that teach about him?

A series of polls in the 1970s and early 1980s was designed to provide insights into these broad questions. One aim was to explore the depths of commitment of professed Christians, but attention was also given to the views of non-Christians —skeptics, agnostics, atheists—because our society is pluralistic, and freedom to practice one's beliefs is a cherished right.

For concerned U.S. Christians, the results provide a mixed bag. On the one hand, the polls of the 1980s indicate a growing spiritual awareness when compared with earlier studies. On the other, this awareness didn't seem to be reflected in adherence to Christ's teachings or in church membership, attendance, and participation.

Both the polls and the verbalized follow-up interviews show that there are significant differences in the ways that Jesus has influenced Americans' lives.

We will summarize some chief findings, first of the statistical data, then of the open-ended interviews.

• In terms of happiness with their lives, spiritually committed Christians are significantly more likely to say that they are "very happy" than is the public at large.

• Age appears to be a significant factor. The older an American is the more likely he or she is to feel that Jesus has influenced his or her life. While this might be expected, the percentage of those who acknowledge a "great impact" rises quite spectacularly from the 18-to-24 age group to the over-65s.

• Women are more likely than men to feel that Jesus' teachings have influenced their lives.

• Married persons are more likely to see significant influence than singles.

• Denomination is also a factor. Protestants are more apt than Catholics to acknowledge a "great impact" and Jews and nonbelievers a much lesser one, if any.

• Nonwhites, significantly more than whites, say that their understanding of Christianity has influenced them deeply.

• On a regional basis, Southerners are much more likely than Northerners or Westerners to acknowledge that Jesus or their church has affected them significantly.

• A high percentage of Americans think that membership in a local church is significantly less important in being a follower of Christ than is obedience to the Ten Commandments or any of several other criteria.

A basic and wide-ranging question in the studies of perceptions of Jesus asked:

What impact would you say Jesus, as a moral and ethical teacher, has had on your life?

As many as 61 percent replied that Jesus, as a moral and ethical teacher, had had a "great" impact on them. Another 26 percent answered "some," making a total of 87 percent who acknowledged a Christian influence. Few—only 7 percent—responded "hardly any" or "none," while 6 percent voiced "no opinion."

Understandably, among those who agree that "Jesus was God," some 79 percent said that as a teacher he had had a "great impact," and another 18 percent acknowledged "some impact." Only 3 percent of those who believed in his divinity replied "hardly any," "none," or "no opinion."

Breakdowns of responses to this question by age, group, gender, and marital status, however, produce interesting and significant results.

Only 41 percent of young Americans between the ages of 18 and 24 cite a "great" impact, as compared with almost 58 percent in the 25-to-29 group, 62 percent in the 30-to-49 group, 67 percent in the 50-to-64 category, and 74 percent in the 65-and-over group.

This rising curve from youth to age is not in itself unusual. Traditionally, young people reject the values of their parents and elders, to some extent, but often return to them as they mature. However, when combined with the results of other findings, the discrepancy can be considered significant.

In addition, more women (67 percent) perceive a "great" impact than men (55 percent), but men (31 percent) are more likely than women (22 percent) to acknowledge "some" impact.

Marital status also seems to be a factor. Married persons (65 percent) report a "great" impact more than singles (44 percent). Interestingly, however, the highest percentage in this category involves those who are divorced, separated, or widowed (67 percent). We can only speculate about the reasons. While married persons are shown to be highly influenced by Jesus' teachings, the divorced, separated, and widowed are even more so. Pastoral counselors conjecture that feelings of loneliness, bereavement, remorse, and even guilt are factors, but whatever the reasons these people appear to find solace in Christ's teachings. It is a matter for clergy and other Christians to ponder. (See Table 13.)

Taking the basic question of Jesus' impact as a moral and ethical teacher a step farther, pollsters asked:

Do you consider yourself to be a Christian?

Eighty-seven percent had previously acknowledged "great" or "some" impact by Jesus as a teacher. The percentage shrank somewhat with this question. Eighty-one percent of Americans surveyed indicated that they classified themselves as Christians or were undecided (7 percent). The remaining 12 percent replied that they were not Christians. Among spiritually committed Americans, some 93 percent call themselves Christians, and this proportion is highest among those who believe that their relationship to Jesus greatly increases their feelings of self-worth (96 percent) and those who are striving greatly to follow Jesus' example (98 percent).

Obviously, many of the less spiritually committed groups must consider themselves Christians, since 81 percent so classify themselves. Some 61 percent of non-church members, 58 percent of those who see little or no value in their relationship with Jesus, 51 percent of those making little or no effort to follow his example, and 50 percent of those who do not believe Jesus was divine or who even doubt his historical existence consider themselves Christians. So, too, do 45 percent of those who feel religion is not very important in their lives.

Age is also a factor in self-classification. A significantly smaller proportion in the younger age groups consider themselves Christians than do those in the older categories, and women are more likely to do so than men, but the margin is not as wide. (See Table 14.)

Just what is a true Christian in American eyes?

Any effort to assess Jesus' impact should come to grips with that question. If we accept the premise that "a faith unlived is no faith at all" and that a large majority of Americans consider themselves Christians, a workable definition of just what they mean by "Christian" is in order.

A representative cross section was asked:

Of the statements on this card, which four do you think are the most important if someone is trying to be a follower of Jesus?

Sixteen possible responses were listed, which represent a fairly wide range of concepts:

Obeying the Ten Commandments

Forgiving those who have wronged you

Putting others' needs before your own

Living in such a way as to draw others to Jesus

Person-to-person charitable activities among the under-privileged, the sick, the elderly

Consoling those in sorrow or affliction

Telling people about Jesus

Being active in a local church

Studying the Bible daily

Having a regular prayer time

Counseling and praying with those who need support and encouragement

Being cheerful in every situation

Receiving Holy Communion

Becoming involved in community activities

Working for social justice

Don't know

The responses most frequently mentioned were obeying the Ten Commandments, forgiving those who have wronged you, putting others' needs before your own, and living in such a way as to draw others to Jesus. These four were mentioned by more than 3 in 10 of the public at large, including nearly half (48 percent) of those who said they were living by the Ten Commandments. Among spiritually committed individuals, 4 in 10 or more mention most of these, and more than half cite the first one —obeying the Ten Commandments.

About 1 in 4 mentioned that person-to-person charitable activities (23 percent) were important. Consoling those who are in sorrow or affliction was also cited by 23 percent, telling people about Jesus by 22 percent, being active in a local church by 20 percent, studying the Bible daily by 19 percent, and having a regular prayer time by 19 percent. Interestingly, these last four were mentioned by higher percentages (one quarter to one third) of Americans with greater spiritual commitments.

Less important (mentioned by 17 percent or less of all respondents and those showing religious commitment) were counseling and praying with those who need support and encouragement (17 percent), being cheerful in every situation (17 percent), receiving Holy Communion (14 percent), becoming involved in community activities (10 percent), and working for social justice (10 percent). (See Table 15.)

"Obeying the Ten Commandments" led the list of criteria for being a follower of Jesus. The Decalogue, of course, was the divine law given Moses in the Old Testament accounts and formed the basis of much of the ethical and moral codes of Christianity, Judaism, and Islam, as well as many of our civil laws. Jesus summarized ten into two: love God, and love your neighbor as yourself (Matt. 22:37–40).

A poll question sought to discover the relative importance Americans attach to the first two commandments. Asked: **Which comes closer to how you feel?** 64 percent said love of God, but a significant minority of 11 percent felt the opposite. And an even more significant minority of 17 percent volunteered the opinion that they were equally important.

Among the more religiously involved respondents, the proportions believing love of God comes before love of neighbor were larger than those of the general public, and the percentages expressing the other opinions were correspondingly smaller. For example, of those who believe that their relationship with God enhances their self-worth greatly, 83 percent gave love of God preference, as against only 3 percent who cited love of neighbor and 13 percent who considered them equal. (See Table 16.)

Because Jesus and his teachings have influenced a substantial majority of Americans, they were asked:
In what ways, if any, is Jesus entering or has entered your life, or is having an effect on your life?
Fourteen percent reported that Jesus had had no effect on their lives, and another 22 percent replied, "Don't know."

The remaining respondents—and they total more than 100 percent because of multiple answers—cited a variety of ways. Ten percent noted that Jesus "helped or guided me," 9 percent said that he had "set an example for me to follow," 8 percent cited "helped during illness" or "gave me health," and 8 percent said he had "helped me have compassion."

If combined and taken together, an impressive 25 percent noted effects that related to attitudes and general happiness. Seven percent said that he had "improved my outlook and thinking," 6 percent found he had "helped me have peace and calmed me," another 6 percent said "his teachings have helped me be a better person," 3 percent cited that he made them "feel better and happier," as did 3 percent who said that "he gave me courage."

Americans with stronger Christian convictions than the public at large mentioned the same sorts of ways that Jesus had entered their lives, but with somewhat greater frequency.

In the sample as a whole, whereas 14 percent reported no effect on their lives, among those with a spiritual commitment, only 6 percent so responded. (See Table 17.)

If "a faith unlived is no faith at all," how one lives one's life according to the values and principles of one's religion or philosophy is a good yardstick for measuring one's commitment to its tenets. A survey question asked:

How hard have you tried to follow the example of Jesus —if at all?

This question—more subjective than most of the others— required very subjective answers. One person's "greatest possible effort" might be another's "some effort." Viewed objectively, both might be considered to be doing the same thing. Nonetheless, the responses can be revealing.

About 79 percent—roughly 130 million adults—reported that they were making at least *some* effort to follow the example of Christ. However, the proportion making the "greatest effort possible" was small (12 percent, or 1 in 8), while one third (33 percent) reported "considerable" effort and another 34 percent said "some" effort. Only 5 percent reported that they were making "no effort at all."

More likely than the average to be making the "greatest possible effort" were Protestants (especially Baptists), nonwhites, those with only a grade-school education, and women. And younger respondents were less likely than older Americans to be making the "greatest" effort or "considerable" effort to follow his example. (See Table 18.)

Another related and highly subjective question asked:

How close do you feel you yourself come in following the example of Jesus?

The results indicate that Americans are sanguine about how close they are coming to following Jesus' example. Fifty-seven percent think they are coming at least "fairly close," including

10 percent who said "very close." One third, however, are less positive: 26 percent said they were "not very close" and another 8 percent "not at all close."

Cross-tabulating these responses against those given to the question on the "effort" individuals were making indicates somewhat the same consistent pattern: The greater the effort, the closer Americans feel they are coming to following his example. For instance, 44 percent of those who feel they are making the greatest effort feel they are coming "very close," as against only 4 percent of those making "some effort" and 1 percent of those making hardly any or no effort. Similarly, the proportion who feel they are "not very close" is small (6 percent) among those making the "greatest effort possible" and large (41 percent) among those making only "some" effort. (See Table 19.)

A test of faith, of course, is how faith is put into action, but commitment can take many forms. An Albert Schweitzer can serve as a medical missionary in tropical Africa, a Mother Teresa can minister to the poor in the slums of Calcutta, a cloistered nun can devote her life to prayer, and an inspired evangelist can preach the gospel. But these are dramatic examples. Few Americans—even committed Christians—are called to demonstrate their faith so intensely, yet the influence of Jesus can be assessed by their deeds.

Love, which Paul said was greater even than faith and hope, tells something of how individuals translate their feelings about Christ into action. The question asked:

How often, if at all, during the past year have you done each of the following?

Five categories of charitable or volunteer work were listed. A majority of those questioned reported having donated time to help someone (other than a family member) who was sick or in need, but only a minority—2 in 5—said they had ever done volunteer work at their church. (See Table 20.)

Of the 38 percent of the public at large who had done volunteer work at least once during the preceding year, statistics showed that the proportions were highest among church members and those for whom religion is very important (about half the respondents), and those who believe Jesus was God (just under half). These proportions are especially high among respondents who believe that their relationship with Jesus increases their self-worth a great deal and among those making the greatest possible effort to follow Jesus' example.

Most psychologists would agree that one's happiness or unhappiness is shaped by how one feels about oneself. Self-esteem, self-image, self-worth, self-respect—whatever the term, it is a major factor. Since Jesus and Christianity have influenced Americans' views, how have their relationships with Jesus affected their feelings about themselves? Americans were asked:

To what extent, if at all, does your relationship with Jesus increase your sense of self-worth—that is, make you feel better about yourself?

As a whole, some 36 percent of the American public felt that their self-esteem was enhanced "a great deal" and another 37 percent replied "somewhat." Among the spiritually committed the positive percentages rose sharply to a high of 78 percent among those making the greatest possible effort to follow Jesus' example. (See Table 21.)

There are many phenomena that humans believe, sense, or feel but cannot prove in a purely scientific sense: superstitions, fantasies, theories. Many Americans, for instance, believe in extrasensory perception (ESP), a mysterious telepathic force that allows communication between humans. But despite decades of research, psychologists can neither categorically prove nor disprove that it exists.

There is no scientifically provable reproducible evidence that Jesus is alive in heaven and that he exerts an influence—a benign influence—on Americans today. Yet many Americans attest that they think so.

A poll question asked:

Have you sensed Jesus' presence?

More than half of spiritually committed Americans have sensed Jesus' presence "often" in various situations. Several categories were suggested by the questioner, such as in nature, in times of personal crisis, and in church or during religious services.

The proportions were highest among those who think that their relationship with Jesus greatly increases their self-worth and those who are making the greatest possible effort to follow his example. Among the group with increased self-worth, for instance, 68 percent (some 2 in 3) have sensed Jesus' presence often in nature, 76 percent in times of personal crisis, and 75 percent during church or religious services. (See Table 22.)

The impact that Jesus has had on Americans is manifested dramatically in the so-called "born-again" experience. This is usually defined as a turning point in life in which the subject commits himself or herself to Jesus. The phrase derives from Jesus' admonition in the New Testament (John 3:3), "Except a man be born again, he cannot see the kingdom of God" (KJV).

As former President Jimmy Carter, himself an avowed born-again Christian, put it, "We believe that the first time we're born, as children, it's human life that is given to us; and when we accept Jesus as our Savior, it's a new life."

And Jesus said, "That which is born of the flesh is flesh; and that which is born of the Spirit is spirit." The Gospel continues, "The wind bloweth where it listeth, and thou hearest the sound thereof, but canst not tell whence it cometh, and whither it goeth; so is every one that is born of the spirit" (John 3:6, 8, KJV).

The experience takes many forms and varies in intensity. For Saul of Tarsus, the persecutor of Christians in biblical times who became the apostle Paul, it was a vision of Christ crucified; for others of subsequent generations it could be a gradual awakening and acceptance.

One survey asked Americans:

Would you say that you have been born again or have had a born-again experience—that is, a turning point in your life when you committed yourself to Jesus Christ? Was this a sudden experience, a gradual experience, or both?

Nearly two out of five Americans (38 percent) reported having the born-again experience (a rather remarkable percentage); 53 percent reported not.

Those with spiritual commitments reported such experiences with greater frequency. Those making the greatest possible effort to follow Jesus reported it in 76 percent of cases, as did 55 percent of those to whom religion was very important. Of the 38 percent who reported the experience, most said it had been a gradual change rather than a sudden one.

As in responses to some previous questions, women (43 percent) were more likely than men (32 percent), the elderly more than the young, the married (40 percent) more than the single (30 percent), and nonwhites (51 percent) more than whites (35 percent) to report the experience. Protestants (52 percent) were overwhelmingly more apt than Catholics (21 percent) to say they had had the experience. This may be due in some part to the greater emphasis that some Protestant denominations place on born-again experiences. (See Tables 23 and 24.)

Another—and related—phenomenon is the so-called "near-death experience." While both are mystical phenomena, those who have experienced the latter are much less likely to see Christ as the center of their life.

In the past fifteen years or so the near-death experience (NDE) has been the subject of intense scientific investigation by psychiatrists, psychologists, and medical researchers. Modern medical techniques and resuscitation methods have brought back to life many people who were considered clinically and legally dead. They may have had no heartbeat, were not breathing, and had no detectable brain function. Yet they survived.

When they returned from this state to consciousness, a significant number reported having vivid experiences while on the threshold of death. Their accounts were startlingly similar and could not be easily explained away or dismissed as mere coincidence.

For most of the survivors it was an intensely spiritual experience. Had they had a glimpse into the beyond? Humans, almost from the beginnings of history, have been fascinated by the possibility of an afterlife, an existence that continues after an earthly death. The idea has been the basis of many of the world's religions and certainly of Christianity. Jesus' resurrection and his promise of eternal life are its centerpiece.

Do those who recount these vivid experiences actually have a brief look into the future that lies ahead for all of us?

Jesus Christ and his role in Americans' lives today is the focus of this book. How does he figure in the philosophy of those who may—or may not—have had that glimpse?

The Gallup Organization conducted surveys in the early 1980s to determine the extent and intensity of the NDE.

The results of interviews with 1,750 representative Americans, when projected for the entire U.S. public, indicated that an astounding 23 million had had at least some of the experiences associated with the phenomenon. And of that 23 million, some 8 million had had what came to be known as the "core experience"—that is, had felt most of the patterns or ideas that the experiencers had in common.

A typical core experience was described by Raymond A. Moody, Jr., in his book *Life After Life:*

> A man is dying and, as he reaches the point of greatest physical distress, he hears himself pronounced dead by his doctor. He begins to hear an uncomfortable noise, a loud ringing or buzzing, and at the same time feels himself moving very rapidly through a long dark tunnel. After this, he suddenly finds himself outside of his own physical body, but still in the immediate physical environment, and he sees his own body from a distance, as though he is a spectator. He watches the resuscitation attempt from this unusual vantage point and is in a state of emotional upheaval.
>
> After a while, he collects himself and becomes more accustomed to his odd condition. He notices that he still has a "body," but one of a very different nature and with very different powers from the physical body he has left behind. Soon . . . others come to meet and to help him. He glimpses the spirits of relatives and friends who have already died, and a loving, warm spirit of a kind he has never encountered before—a being of light—appears before him. This being asks him a question, nonverbally, to make him evaluate his life and helps him along by showing him a panoramic, instantaneous playback of the major events of his life. At some point he finds himself approaching some sort of barrier or border, apparently representing the limit between earthly life and the next life. Yet, he finds that he must go back to the earth, that the time for his death has not yet come. At this point he resists, for by now he is taken up with his experiences in the afterlife and does not want to return. He is overwhelmed by intense feelings of joy, love, and peace. Despite his attitude, though, he somehow reunites with his physical body and lives. . . .
>
> The experience affects his life profoundly, especially his views about death and its relationship to life.

There are many doubters, of course, skeptics who deny or question the validity of the accounts and consider them trauma-induced hallucinations or dreams. But as one near-death survivor has said (and his reaction is typical), "If I have a dream, chances are that I can't remember the main features ten minutes later, much less the details. After fifteen years I can recall in great detail everything about that day. And the details never change. It's as vivid as ever."

Examining the statistical data and assessing the interview impressions of the impact Jesus has on Americans today provides clear indications that people are more concerned with the here-and-now than with the hereafter. Concerns about an afterlife were voiced less often, but underlying earthly concerns is a concept of divine justice, a feeling that injustices perpetrated on earth will be rectified in an afterlife by an omnipotent, all-knowing God. Christ's mission, according to Christian theology, was to offer redemption and entry to heaven through his sacrifice.

How, then, does the intense experience affect the near-death survivors in their relationship to Jesus? The Presence or Being of Light that they felt seemed loving, forgiving, and compassionate, all qualities noted in the Gospels and ascribed by Americans to Jesus.

But the Presence or Being of Light was seldom identified as Jesus, even among those with strong Christian backgrounds. In fact, one study indicated that those with Christian backgrounds constituted a minority of those who have had the core experience. Such things as a born-again experience or other religious awakening or a religious commitment are by no means prerequisites to having the classical verge-of-death encounter. It is as likely to happen to those with little or no religious orientation as it is to those who are very religious.

Kenneth Ring, a respected investigator of the near-death experience, has reported similar findings. Ring is professor of psychology at the University of Connecticut, president of the International Association for Near-Death Studies, and author of two widely hailed books on the subject. While his sample base was narrower than the Gallup Organization's, he found very few who identified the Presence as Jesus and none who said that the Being of Light *identified himself* as Christ. Some felt that they were in the presence of God, but the overall impression of the Being of Light was that it was a kind of universal spirit.

And when asked if they believed that eternal life is available only to those who believe in Jesus as Lord and Savior, the near-death survivors were twice as likely to reject the idea as those who had not had the experience.

An overwhelming majority of those willing to talk about their near-death experience saw the "other side" as a place of joy, peace, and love. However, a small minority of those who discussed it saw another picture—one of darkness, fire, torment, and pain.

The various polls and statistics relating to Jesus' influence on people's lives provide the big picture, but this is made up of many "little pictures" that can provide useful insights and illuminate an issue.

A general's view of a battle scene is quite different from that of the privates at the front, but the plan of battle will only be successful if the general understands the privates' inner convictions and can inspire and motivate them. Similarly, each private's attitude will be profoundly affected by individual perceptions of the battle plan and a personal belief in the cause.

The analogy between statistical data (the big picture) and open-ended interviews (the little picture) and the military is not perfect, but it can be serviceable. In-depth interviews, while less scientifically representative of the general populace, reinforce much of the statistical data and also reveal some additional human dimensions as to how and why their feelings about Jesus have affected their lives.

Asked to tell in their own words how Jesus had affected their lives, the respondees' answers ranged from terse and cryptic to lengthy and detailed. Some were vague and noncommittal, others were negative, but by and large they reinforced the statistical data.

Many focused on the here-and-now rather than the hereafter. Mentioned often were family concerns such as health, spouse, and children. Many also cited peace of mind and serenity as important. Enhanced self-esteem or feelings of self-worth and the ability to cope with everyday problems were also described frequently. Most dramatic and compelling, however, were the stories of how lives had been completely turned around by newfound faith.

Roughly the same percentage (about 1 in 10) who expressed disbelief or doubts about Jesus responded negatively. For instance, a thirty-four-year-old Mountain View, California, man said cynically, "He's having an effect on my life, all right, but only indirectly, by affecting others. A detrimental effect, I might add." And a forty-three-year-old Kewanee, Illinois, man replied, "I don't feel that Jesus has had any effect at all."

A twenty-nine-year-old man from San Jose, California, said, "I'm really not affected very much by Jesus. I believe in God, but I'm not a born-again Christian or Jesus freak or anything like that."

Some ambivalence was expressed by a forty-eight-year-old Colts Neck, New Jersey, man. "My freedom has been denied because society has made laws based on religious beliefs. But I can also see that religious beliefs have made people more sensitive to the needs of others." Pressed to explain or offer examples, he declined. "Let it stand at that," he said.

A thirty-year-old East Dayton, Ohio, man said, "As a result of having read and being familiar with his teachings I have been influenced. But I use them as moral guides. His ideas have influenced society for the better. However, I follow them out of respect for the *logic* of the beliefs, rather than their divinity."

Those views are in a minority, however. Firm believers, like a fifty-one-year-old Georgetown, South Carolina, woman, for example, said that Jesus had influenced her deeply "by answering my prayers. I've seen people healed by prayer, even my husband. . . . With Jesus you have someone to go to when you have a problem. You're never alone."

A thirty-seven-year-old well-educated Bostonian answered the question with another question. "What else is there to believe in except God and Jesus the Redeemer?" He had attended parochial school but—as he put it—"tuned out" in high school and college. "But when I became a family man I had to rethink a lot of things. I read a lot and talked to others a lot, but the things I had learned in my childhood stood up. What is it the Jesuits say, 'Give us a child until age eight . . . '?"

A thirty-six-year-old Tampa, Florida, woman responded by pointing to her two children and saying, "I've had three deaths in the family in the past year and only because of the Lord can I accept that. But I do have these two."

A thirty-two-year-old Fort Worth, Texas, man replied, "Jesus has made me more understanding of God's will for us. It's hard to understand why my twelve-year-old daughter died, but I now recognize that God knows best."

A twenty-two-year-old Elizabeth, West Virginia, man said, "He has uplifted my spirit and brought my family closer together. He has shown me what children are for."

A thirty-four-year-old man from Flagstaff, Arizona, a member of the Church of Jesus Christ of Latter-day Saints, said, "Through the church I've learned to be a better husband and parent, to utilize my priesthood and improve my character. It [my belief] brought me to a closer understanding of Jesus and the will of God."

And a thirty-one-year-old Sissonville, West Virginia, woman said that initially her feelings about Jesus came through her husband. "He's a new Christian and I've seen how God has changed his life. That has affected my life. I'm seeking a better understanding of him, and I think I'm coming closer."

Some others have found that Jesus and Christianity can help them to help others.

One such is a thirty-eight-year-old black man, a physical education teacher and coach at an inner-city New York high school. "The kids here need role models," he said. "They are into sports and show business because they see that these are fields where blacks can make big bucks and be heroes." Unfortunately, he added, only one in maybe fifty varsity athletes will get an athletic scholarship to college and maybe one in a thousand will make it to the pros. The odds on a show business career are even longer.

For whatever reasons, the kids tend to respect the views of athletic coaches, he said, and "we try to encourage them to do their best in the classrooms as well as on the athletic fields."

Some of the role models they see are drug pushers and pimps, and it's "pretty tempting.

"We've had some visitors from groups like the Fellowship of Christian Athletes and others who have emphasized what religion has meant to them in their careers and their personal lives. The point is that these guys—ones with a religious commitment —*are winners, both on and off the field.* The students tend to look up to them and copy them," he explained.

He noted that he had often watched Dr. Schuller's *Hour of*

Power TV program. (He had been told that Dr. Schuller was involved in the survey.)

"I started watching the program because he comes on here [in New York] just before the Sunday ball games. I liked the music and his message, and some of his interviews with sports people I've seen like outfielder Andre Thornton, pitcher Tommy John, Roger Staubach [former Dallas Cowboys quarterback] and some others give me something to pass on to the kids. It helps."

But the most dramatic responses to the question of "impact on your life" came from some who had hit bottom emotionally, physically, and spiritually and then recovered and found their way through faith in Jesus. They tend to be candid and open and talk about their experiences with great conviction and intensity.

A typical response was volunteered by a forty-four-year-old ex-hippie, now a bus driver in New Hampshire:

"What impact has he [Jesus] had on me? He turned my whole life around. I make a living driving a bus, but Jesus is my life."

Larry (not his real name) is a born-again Christian, one of the 38 percent of Americans who so classify themselves. Unmarried, he is a member of a fundamentalist church and now devotes much of his free time to church affairs and evangelism.

A son of comfortably well-off parents, he attended excellent schools but became a college dropout. His college program combined academic studies with work experience, and he found himself assigned to a national broadcasting network's headquarters in New York City as—as he termed it—"a gofer, a glorified flunky." He was lonely in the city and found himself drifting and drawn to the Greenwich Village scene. There he met a "strange crowd" and was introduced to marijuana and hallucinogens like LSD.

"I was a buttoned-down flunky by day and a Village bohemian by night," he said. He was unhappy and even considered suicide. A psychiatrist was not much help, so he took the "geographic cure." He bought a motorcycle and rode it to San Francisco, where the Haight-Ashbury drug scene was in flower. He also had a romantic notion that he could bike from San Francisco to the southern tip of South America and qualify for the *Guinness Book of World Records*.

A little sober examination of the hazards of motorcycle travel through Central and South America and a growing disillusionment with San Francisco prompted him to travel to New Mexico to look over the hippie communes there. He wasn't fully accepted, but he stayed on the fringes of several groups, especially one called the Jesus Movement. There he found some companionship, but not conviction or conversion.

The exposure to believing Christians apparently had an effect, however. In September 1970, while on a drug-buying mission to neighboring Arizona, he was involved in an automobile accident. He was asleep in the back seat and suffered a broken shoulder and other injuries.

At the time he was under indictment for forging a $50 check that he had used to buy stereo sound equipment. He realized that he could also be charged with illegal flight to avoid prosecution if he had crossed the Arizona border.

Hospitalized and filled with fear and self-pity, he was near despair when about fifteen members of the Jesus Movement group appeared in his hospital room and asked him to pray with them.

"That's when I turned my life over to Christ," he said. "It wasn't a sudden, dramatic thing, like Saul's conversion on the road to Damascus, but it was the beginning."

He saw some symbolism in the experience. "I had just turned thirty that day, and Jesus began his public ministry at age thirty," he said. "I had been hospitalized for three days, dead in mind and spirit, you might say. And, of course, Christ rose from the dead after three days. I thought about that a lot, and prayed and meditated, but it took me a couple of years to get my head really straight."

He is happy and intense about his new life, but he retains a sense of humor about his former life-style. "I didn't brush my teeth for three years and took baths very infrequently. That should tell you something about how I lived. My folks had no idea whether I was alive or dead. They hired an agency to track me down but had no luck. At Christmastime—if I thought about it—I'd send them a postcard. They've been very supportive of me in my new life, and I love them very much. I always have, I suppose.

"How would I rank my efforts to follow Jesus' example? On

a scale of one to ten, about a five. I've got a long way to go to reach his perfection."

The drug culture types that he encountered often turned around the Marxist aphorism, "Religion is the opiate of the people," he said. They made it: "Opiates are the religion of the people."

5

What Can Opinion Research Teach Us?

I do not claim that I have already succeeded or have already become perfect. I keep striving to win the prize for which Christ Jesus has already won me to himself. Of course, my brothers, I really do not think that I have already won it; the one thing I do, however, is to forget what is behind me and do my best to reach what is ahead. So I run straight toward the goal in order to win the prize, which is God's call through Christ Jesus to the life above.

—Philippians 3:12–14

Americans tend to be pragmatists. Confronted by a problem they are more likely to try to come to grips with it, in the conviction that they can change things, than stand around wringing their hands. And American Christians are likely to want to share their faith with others, so this is a challenge for them.

What can committed Christians—both clergy and laity—do? Many, like Dr. Schuller, who commissioned some of the basic studies described here, feel that churches must take a new and careful look at what they are doing—or not doing. He has called for a "New Reformation," a reassessment of what churches can do to "go forth and teach all nations." Both knowledge and leadership are clearly indicated.

The salesmen in that delightful musical comedy *The Music Man* chorused, "You gotta know the territory." The thought has become a cliché among those whose jobs entail persuasion, but like most clichés it contains a kernel of truth. Can opinion research help Christians understand their "territory"?

Former President Harry S. Truman took a dim view of poll

results. This was understandable because in his presidential race against Governor Thomas E. Dewey in 1948 the polls indicated that he would be defeated. In *Off the Record,* a recently published collection of his private papers edited by Robert H. Ferrell (Harper & Row, 1980), he wrote:

> I wonder how far Moses would have gone if he'd taken a poll in Egypt? What would Jesus Christ have preached if he'd taken a poll in Israel? Where would the Reformation have gone if Martin Luther had taken a poll? It isn't polls or public opinion of the moment that count. It is right and wrong and leadership—men with fortitude, honesty, and a belief in the right that makes epochs in the history of the world.

Both the salesmen and President Truman were right in their own ways. President Truman was both right and fortunate. He could exert leadership because America was then at the peak of its international political and economic influence, and Harry really did sense the country's mood and know just how far he could go.

Good leaders, whether they be Moses, Jesus, Paul, Augustine, Luther, Calvin, or whoever, not only had to understand and expound their beliefs but also to know their audiences and the times in which they lived.

It is our hope, then, that the data and commentary presented here will help Jesus' followers in their search for knowledge of him and his teachings.

Previous chapters have focused sharply on perceptions of Jesus, both today and over the ages, and how these concepts affect Christians in their personal lives and in their roles as members of society.

Modern opinion polls isolate a single movement or action in a single moment of time. They are most useful when contrasted with other periods and when perspectives and trends can be established.

Fortunately for our purposes, attitudes toward Jesus seldom change substantially overnight, but they do change, and the changes can be revealing. Unfortunately, American media often seize on a single transitory blip indicated on the computer readouts and magnify it to cosmic proportions.

Our polls have focused on Jesus. The Old Testament teachings have their place in Christianity, but Jesus is the centerpiece. Churches can and should be the media to spread his message.

How are they doing?

There are essentially two dimensions to what believing Christians are asked to do: (1) foster and advance belief in God and in Jesus as Redeemer and messenger to humankind and (2) provide guidance and a sense of community that enable people to live together in harmony according to his precepts.

Numerous surveys have shown that religion can make a profound difference, both in the lives of individuals and in the quality of their society. Religiously involved Americans tend to develop stronger family ties than the noncommitted, to be more actively involved in charitable activities and community affairs. They are more likely also to have a positive outlook and to have discovered clear-cut goals and a satisfying purpose in life.

As they affect churches, some recent statistics, when compared with data from earlier surveys, indicate some interesting and sometimes contradictory points:

• 4 in 5 Americans (81 percent) classify themselves as Christians.

• 7 in 10 Americans (71 percent) say they are members of a church or synagogue, down 5 percentage points from the 1947 high of 76 percent.

• 2 in 5 (42 percent) of Americans attend church services in a given week, down from a high of 49 percent in the mid-1950s.

Although 4 of 5 Americans classify themselves as Christians, only about 2 in 5 of the respondents (42 percent) knew that Jesus delivered the Sermon on the Mount, only 46 percent could name the first four books of the New Testament, 45 percent could name fewer than half of the Ten Commandments, and only a disappointing 70 percent knew that Jesus was born in Bethlehem. Paradoxically, perhaps, despite surveys that showed more regular church attendance in the mid-1950s than in the mid-1980s, Americans' knowledge of these basic biblical facts has improved slightly. (See Tables 25–27.)

Another poll result that should dismay clergy and church members is the finding that church membership has a low priority for most Americans. Even among spiritually committed individuals, "being active in a local church" was not a significant concern. Of those to whom religion was very important, 24 percent listed church activity as one of their four choices; individuals who said they were making "the greatest possible effort to follow Jesus' example" noted it by a mere 27 percent. (See Table 15 and chapter 4.)

And while Catholics lead other denominations in regular church attendance, they are less likely (16 percent) than Protestants (24 percent) to feel that being active in church activities is important.

There were significant differences in the importance attached to church activities in breakdowns by gender and marital status (married, single, divorced, separated, or widowed).

Age also appears to be a factor. One in four (25 percent) of those 65 and older deemed church involvement important, while only 15 percent in the 30-to-49 age group agreed.

Among major Protestant denominations, Methodists (35 percent) were most likely to consider church activities important. They were followed by Southern Baptists (27 percent), Lutherans (23 percent), and Baptists (21 percent).

By region the Midwest (22 percent) and the South (22 percent) mentioned the importance of church activities more frequently than the East (19 percent) and the West (16 percent).

Within the Protestant community, the Baptist churches are the preference of 20 percent of Americans; Methodist, 9 percent; Lutheran, 7 percent; Presbyterian, 2 percent; Episcopalian, 3 percent; United Church of Christ, 2 percent; and the Christian Church (Disciples of Christ), 2 percent. (See Table 11.)

Although religious preferences for each of the five major Protestant groups over the past five years or so are relatively unchanged, recent figures are generally lower than those recorded before 1978. For example, the proportion of adults who consider themselves Methodists, Presbyterians, and Episcopalians has declined by roughly one third.

An analysis of trends in religious preference among age groups is also interesting. Comparing the preferences of the adult population as a whole with various age groups indicates that of those 65 years and older some 66 percent register their preference as Protestant, while 57 percent of all Americans do.

But among the 18-to-24 age group only 52 percent do so. This low percentage rises rapidly for older citizens—to 50 percent among the 25-to-29 group, to 56 percent for those 30 to 49 and 62 percent in the 50-to-64 age group.

An opposite trend is seen among those with a Catholic preference (28 percent of all adults). Younger citizens are more likely than older ones to prefer Catholicism. Among the 65-and-older grouping, only 24 percent list this preference, while in the 30-to-49 group it is 28 percent. But younger adults (18 to 24 years old) register 30 percent.

Significant, too, is the bulge evidence among those who report no religious preference. Young adults in the 18-to-24 and 25-to-29 age brackets report no preference by 12 and 13 percent respectively, twice as often as the over-65s and the teenagers. (See Table 12.)

While religion has a powerful appeal for Americans, probing more deeply through surveys indicates that even if religion is an important force in our lives it is not the center of our lives. It does not have primacy. Interest may be high, but commitment is often low.

The Gallup Organization developed a special scale to determine the level of Americans' spiritual commitment. Based on answers by survey respondents to seven basic questions about their faith, it disclosed that only 12 percent of the populace falls into the category of "highly spiritually committed." Another 37 percent can be considered "fairly high" in commitment, while 36 are "fairly low" and 15 percent rank "very low" in spiritual commitment.

Americans generally rank health, family, love, and friends ahead of religion in their hierarchy of values.

In the 1980s polls have indicated a rising interest in spiritual matters, after years of declining figures. As noted earlier, going-it-alone is an increasing popular approach to God. For example, survey participants were given a card listing seventeen items and asked:

What sort of things, if any, do you do to nourish or strengthen your faith?

Both among all respondents and among those with greater

spiritual commitment, the most frequently cited ways were "pray by oneself," mentioned by 59 percent of the public at large; "help others," mentioned by 51 percent; "attend religious services," 44 percent; and "read the Bible," 39 percent. Among spiritually committed individuals, the percentages are higher. All four of these activities are cited by majorities of the spiritually committed.

Next most frequently cited were "listen to sermons or lectures" (36 percent), "meditation" (32 percent), "take walks" and "seek to commune with nature" (31 percent), "receive Holy Communion" (29 percent), and "watch religious TV programs" (21 percent). (See Table 28.)

A related question asked what emotions they experienced while in a church or synagogue.

In church or synagogue, have you ever felt afraid of God, guilty as a sinner, close to God, or that you are a wonderful person?

In church or synagogue, most Americans do *not* feel afraid of God (78 percent), and most also feel close to him (80 percent).

However, there is a narrower division on the other sentiments. A majority (52 percent) feel conscious of their guilt as sinners when in a church or synagogue; fewer (42 percent) do not feel guilty as sinners. Forty percent feel that they are *not* wonderful persons when in a place of worship. That's only slightly outweighed by the 47 percent who do. Thirteen percent expressed no opinion.

Fear of God while in church was expressed by roughly the same proportion of Americans as a whole as by those who believe Jesus was God and those who felt that their relationship with Jesus increased their feelings of self-worth a lot.

Marked differences are apparent, however, in these groups' feelings of guilt as sinners and closeness to God. Higher proportions (62 percent of both groups) feel conscious of their guilt as sinners as against 52 percent of all Americans.

Analogously, the proportions of these groups who feel close to God while in church are very high: 90 percent of those who believe Jesus was God feel close to God, as do 95 percent of those who feel their self-worth is increased substantially by their relationship with Jesus Christ. In addition, an above-average proportion of the latter group (61 percent) feel they are wonderful persons when in a house of worship.

Among Americans who report that they are making the greatest possible effort to follow Jesus' example, nearly all (98 percent) feel close to God while in church, and 65 percent feel they are wonderful persons while in a house of worship. They are also more likely to feel that they are wonderful persons, and they exhibit only the guilt feelings of the public at large. (See Table 29.)

Evangelizing, spreading the good news of Jesus, is another important aspect of Christ's charge to his followers. Americans apparently take it seriously. Survey respondents were asked:

Have you ever tried to encourage someone to believe in Jesus Christ or to accept him as his or her Savior?

A rather amazing 51 percent of *all* Americans replied affirmatively, and the percentage rose dramatically among the more religiously committed. Sixty-nine percent of those to whom religion is very important answered "yes," as did 80 percent of those who feel that their relationship with Jesus greatly increases their sense of self-worth and 83 percent of those who are making the greatest possible effort to follow Jesus' example. And it should be noted that among the religiously committed group there are many who, without openly evangelizing, attract nonbelievers and others through the power of example and the quality of their lives. The survey data clearly indicate that a concerned laity can be a powerful influence in church affairs. (See Table 30.)

What does the public feel churches could do for them? The question was asked:

In which of these ways, if any, would you like to see churches serve you better?

Respondents were shown cards with 8 optional replies. Of the total responses, three were mentioned by at least 1 out of 3. "Help you put your faith into practice" (37 percent), "Enable you to deepen your relationship with Jesus Christ" (35 percent), and "Shed light on issues such as the problems of suffering, death, and dying" (33 percent). Close behind were "Help people to be more effective parents" (32 percent) and "Enable you to serve others better" (31 percent).

Among the more religiously committed, a bare majority mentioned the first two options.

And 1 in 5 of the total sample mentioned that churches would serve better by helping them develop greater use of their talents (21 percent) or helping them in their prayer life (19 percent).

Among the more religiously involved Americans, about half mentioned helping to put their faith into practice and deepening their relationship with Jesus. (See Table 31.)

Clearly, the responses indicate some confusion, mixed feelings, and tentativeness about the role of churches. While a church should not be controlled by public opinion in terms of doctrine, the mood of the congregation should be weighed if Christian clergymen and concerned laity are to exert the leadership required.

Our polls show that more than 4 in 5 adult Americans consider themselves Christians, but that only about half of them attend church services regularly (once a month or more).

The others are called "unchurched," but they are believers by our definition. Most have some kind of religious background or at least an awareness of religious values. And studies show that at least half of them can see situations that would bring them back to the community of active worshipers.

Studies of the unchurched point to four basic groups as being "open to renewed involvement." Even the "nominally churched" also exhibit many of the same characteristics. The studies show that:

• Family-oriented people want their children to have a religious background and moral teaching. Some 9 in 10—no matter what their own religious commitments—have firm convictions about training for their offspring. Parental attitudes, of course, usually shape their young children's views, and if parents are to be convincing to their kids, they are often drawn to the institutional church.

• Many of the unchurched want to fulfill inner religious needs. For many it is a compelling need, as evidenced by data indicating that most show an interest in growing in their religious faith and would like religion to play a more important role in society in the coming years. Often they see that their religious friends and neighbors have achieved a peace of mind and serenity that they lack.

• There are also those who seek the fellowship or social life that a church or synagogue can afford. In our increasingly urban and impersonal society, many Americans feel lonely and remote from one another. As many as 4 in 10, for example, admit to frequent or occasional spells of intense loneliness.

• There are also those who are genuinely interested in attending worship services but who have not been able to find a house of worship that meets their needs or were turned off by minor doctrinal differences or what they felt was a coolness or indifference by clergy and congregation.

We've seen that there is a rising tide of interest in religious and spiritual matters, even if it is not always manifested in church attendance and activities. Some 3 out of 5 Americans today say that they are more interested in religious matters than they were just five years previously. A majority say they are more reliant on God, and as many as 2 out of 5 say their spiritual well-being has improved.

The "why" of this increased interest is perhaps the most intriguing development for Christians. Those surveyed who say they are more reliant on God cite as their key reasons, a feeling of a closer personal relationship with God, a better understanding of him and his purposes, the frequently depressing world situation and threat of nuclear war, and to some extent a feeling of desperation, as if to ask: "Where else but to God does one turn in times like these?"

Surveys also reveal a growing conviction that religion, rather than science, can answer the problems of the world. Over half the respondents said they are more likely to feel this way than they were five years previously, while only a quarter said "less likely." It would appear that Americans are coming increasingly to believe that world problems will be solved not through technology and social engineering but instead through changing hearts and a turning to God. Americans are clearly searching with a new intensity for spiritual moorings in their lives.

The implications from the point of view of organized mainstream religious institutions is immense. Here is an unprecedented opportunity for the churches to tap this burgeoning interest in religion and channel it into solid spiritual commitment. There is a pronounced urgency in this because the renewed interest in religious matters could take (and in some instances, has taken) bizarre turns and lead to unconventional religions and cults, such as the mass suicides of the Reverend Jim Jones's followers in Guyana in 1978. However, the new interest in religious and spiritual matters we see developing in the United States has not—at least until now—been reflected to any great extent in increased involvement on the national level. Church membership and church attendance continue to remain flat.

Much of what is considered positive about Christianity by American Christians is centered on the person of Jesus. As Dr. Schuller has said, "He is the core of Christianity, and if that core drops away, all else can easily fall away."

To recapitulate some of the major affirmative findings of the foregoing and other polls on today's Americans' perceptions of him:

- A large majority of Americans (70%) see Jesus in a divine context.
- Jesus Christ is seen as a living, indwelling Christ, personal and approachable, not merely a historical figure. A majority of Americans say that they have encountered Jesus Christ in their lives, and almost 2 out of 5 say they had a born-again experience, often a gradual one.
- Americans' image of Jesus as a divinity and a person is not sharply focused, yet he is viewed overwhelmingly in a favorable light, with little difference in perceptions based on age, gender, educational level, and so on.
- Jesus is seen as the ideal role model for both men and women and has a powerful appeal even to those who do not believe in his divinity. Two thirds of all Americans express the conviction that Jesus was "without sin," and almost as many believe that Jesus was perfect in all respects.
- Jesus is seen as personifying selfless love. This is the key attribute ascribed to him. To the devout, his life and death are seen as revealing God's love; other traits ascribed to him are kindness, compassion, and capacity to forgive.

• Whether or not Jesus is viewed in divine terms, the majority feel that Jesus Christ, as a moral and ethical teacher, has had a great impact on their lives. Only 7 percent replied "hardly any" or "none."

• A large proportion of Americans (and even larger proportions among the devout groups in the surveys) seek to come closer to following the example of Jesus Christ, and significant proportions believe their relationship with Jesus to be deepening.

• Most seem to believe that following Jesus is a difficult or impossible task, an unattainable ideal. Only 10 percent of the total sample say that they come "very close" to that ideal.

• Those who say that they are trying hard to follow Jesus are among the most devout in the surveys and are more inclined to believe they come closer to following his example than are those who are not making greater efforts.

The surveys of Jesus' impact also revealed some *negative* aspects, at least from the standpoint of religion and religious institutions: To recapitulate:

• From an orthodox point of view, many of those who consider themselves Christians hold views that are inconsistent with traditional Christian beliefs. Belief in his divinity is a key. While most of those who consider themselves Christians see Jesus in a divine context, a significant proportion apparently find it difficult to believe that Jesus was, in fact, God living among men. And a significant proportion of those who say that they are Christians are less than certain that Jesus was divine, while others hold the belief that one can be a true Christian and not believe in the divinity of Jesus.

• Many say they are making a "considerable effort" to follow Jesus' example, but significant proportions say they are not.

• Many, even among the devout, don't appear to be living their faith; that is, putting it into action. For instance, significant proportions admit that they have not—or have only infrequently —given time to help others who may have been sick or in need in some way.

• Prayer plays an important role in the lives of Christian Americans, but relatively few live a life of prayer, a goal of the truly devout person.

• The surveys reveal a low level of biblical knowledge, even among more religiously committed segments of the population. For example, only about 2 in 5 respondents knew that Jesus, according to the Bible, delivered the Sermon on the Mount. And only about 2 in 5 could name more than five of the Ten Commandments.

This brief summary of survey results leads to another and very basic question: What difference does it make to an individual and to society if one has a high level of spirituality and commitment to Christ's principles?

Deeply religious Christians are sometimes accused of holier-than-thou attitudes, of being smug, more interested in their own spiritual welfare than the good of their neighbors, and even of being to some extent intolerant of those who differ from them in religious persuasions and socioeconomic backgrounds.

The accusations would seem unfounded. Only 1 American in 8 (12 percent) fits into our survey category of "highly spiritually committed," but these respondents differ from the rest in at least four key respects:

1. They are more likely to be satisfied with their lives than the less spiritually committed—and far happier. Some 68 percent of the highly spiritually committed said that they are "very happy," compared with only 30 percent of the highly uncommitted. (See Table 32.)

2. The highly spiritually committed tend to place greater importance on family life than do those in less spiritually committed categories.

3. The highly spiritually committed tend to be more tolerant of persons of different races and religions than are those who are less spiritually committed.

4. The highly spiritually committed Americans are vitally concerned about the betterment of society and are far more involved in charitable activities.

Probably the most remarkable finding about the highly spiritually committed, however, is the fact that they tend to be more "downscale" (as sociologists term it) economically and socially than the population as a whole. Overall, "upscale" groups tend to be happier and more content with their lives than "downscale" groups; they are more tolerant of persons of other races and religions and more involved in charitable activities. But the highly spiritually committed, despite economic and psychological pressures, appear to be living out their Christian faith, and their deep convictions seem to have a transforming effect on their lives.

What do the various surveys' numbers say that could account for the perceived increased interest in religious and spiritual matters, even as the data indicate that formalized religion apparently hasn't fulfilled some deep needs that many Americans feel?

Many factors and conjectures based on the surveys can be cited. Certainly the ever-present threat of nuclear annihilation that makes everyone vulnerable is a factor. In World War II it was said that "there are no atheists in foxholes." In a thermonuclear age, we are all vulnerable; the whole world is a foxhole. Economic stress and our inability to deal with many domestic problems often contribute to a turning inward to draw on our spiritual resources.

And to some extent, this feeling seems to come from disenchantment with some modern life-styles and what appears to be a lack of rules and guidelines.

The media are often blamed for glamorizing the darker side of our society, but they should also be credited with increasing the interest in religion. Newspapers, magazines, book publishers, and especially the electronic media are, in one sense, responding to this heightened interest, while in another sense they are creating it.

One notable manifestation of the increased concern about spiritual matters comes from an unexpected quarter, college students and other teenagers. The teen and college years are usually thought of as times of questioning the values of parents and institutions, a seeking of one's own way. Yet the percentage of the nation's college students who say that religion is very important in their lives rose from 39 percent in 1975 and 1979 to 50 percent in a 1983 Gallup Poll survey. That 50 percent compares with 56 percent of the general population.

Their churchgoing has increased too. Some 39 percent said they attend services weekly, as compared with 34 percent in 1975.

Moreover, the proportion of college youth who said their

religious commitment has become stronger since they entered college was twice that of those who said that it has become weaker. (See Table 33.)

Perhaps most significantly, this increased interest has resulted in burgeoning enrollments in nonrequired elective courses in religion, philosophy, and theology. Until quite recently, and certainly before the campus upheavals of the late 1960s and early 1970s, many private schools required a certain number of academic credits in religion, theology, or philosophy.

A high percentage of America's earliest educational institutions had been founded to train an educated clergy. As they began to attract a more diverse student body, students eager to enter such professions as law, medicine, and education, theology assumed a less important place in curriculums. With the passage of the Morrill Land Grant Act in 1862, state-supported higher education and secular education and vocationalism gained ascendance, both in the new state universities and in many of those established under religious auspices. The Morrill Act provided extensive support for colleges of agriculture and the mechanical arts and revolutionized higher education.

In the period of Vietnam-inspired upheaval, "relevance" became a campus buzzword. Many colleges added courses and even departments in some poorly defined "relevant" academic disciplines, and enrollments in religion courses suffered. The trouble was, according to one college professor:

> Relevance is relative. What may seem the wave of the future today could be tomorrow's dodo bird. Interesting, perhaps, as a little blip in history, but not all that significant in the course of human events.
>
> That's where many students of that generation were shortchanged. They got little perspective on the development of human thought about God, Jesus and our destiny.
>
> It's a "back-to-basics" movement in many ways, the kind of reemphasis on the fundamentals, the three R's that primary and secondary schools have started. I applaud it.

The British poet A. E. Housman spoke for many generations of teenagers when he wrote of youth's bewilderment at facing a puzzling future: "I, a stranger and afraid/In a world I never made."

The world they "never made" implies a youthful conviction that parents and other forebears have made a botch of things. And since the world they would inherit is less than perfect, they would change it immediately to conform to their own values.

The passage from childhood dependence to perilous adult independence is difficult at best. For today's young Christians the transition is doubly difficult. They are passing into a society in which unquestioning obedience to religious authorities as well as parental injunctions have lost force.

If, as our surveys indicate, young persons are more concerned and curious about moral values and spiritual matters today and tend to be more idealistic than their elders, clergy and laity have excellent opportunities to advance their faith.

Jesus, after all, was the quintessential idealist. And as some New Englanders put it, "He practiced his preach"—his preach, of course, being love of God and neighbor.

Channeling youthful idealism and intellectual curiosity into a fuller understanding of his message and a commitment to following his way is a challenge to all Christians. The surveys clearly indicate that youths are trying to tell us something. Parents, clergy, and educators would do well to heed them.

The young are not alone in their searching. In today's highly mobile society, Americans often feel rootless, remote from other people and suspicious of everyone. They fear rejection or just would rather "not get involved."

An urban high-rise apartment dweller may nod hello and even smile at a next-door tenant, but that's about all. A suburban homeowner may seek out a neighbor to discuss a proposed municipal tax levy but seldom to discuss spiritual values. And even in small towns and rural communities, where neighborliness and reaching out have been a cherished American tradition, this spirit is waning.

The fact is that many Americans often feel lonely, and their remoteness and isolation is coupled with the frequently expressed conviction that "people just don't care about each other any more." A solid majority, for instance, believe that people today are less willing to help one another than they were just a decade ago.

6

Voices from Today's World

"Also, the Kingdom of heaven is like this. A man is looking for fine pearls, and when he finds one that is unusually fine, he goes and sells everything he has, and buys that pearl."

—Matthew 13:45–46

Statistical findings and interpretations of those findings can take us just so far. The use of that material requires individual analysis and considerable thought. In chapter 3 the data were supplemented by "voices" from the past, the thoughts of a cross section of thinkers and writers who articulated their perceptions of Jesus and his impact on their lives.

This chapter presents the views of some of our contemporaries who are intensely concerned with the Christian ministry. They represent diverse points of view, but all of them are involved in the life of the church and aware of the directions that Christianity is taking.

One such voice is that of Rev. Arie R. Brouwer. He is general secretary of the National Council of the Churches of Christ in the U.S.A., America's largest ecumenical organization, with thirty-one Protestant and Eastern Orthodox groups as members. Before his election to his present post, he served as a deputy general secretary of the World Council of Churches, general secretary of the Reformed Church in America, and pastor of churches in Michigan and New Jersey.

His own beliefs and his vision of Christianity's future are built on the twin pillars of worship and work.

"The connection between the two is vital," he says. "Our

theology cannot live if it is separated from work or from worship. By doing our theology at the juncture between work and worship, we make it possible for our praise and practice to enrich and express and connect each other so that our lives as Christian persons and Christian communities may have integrity."

But what can churches do now to balance the two and foster this worship-work concept?

To Dr. Brouwer, an effective Christianity starts with worship. "It's the center, and where there is a vital center there is an attraction, both to those who are growing up in the church and to those who are in the church. It's important for them to feel what is happening is truly important, not just because they believe it but because they experience it. And if one doesn't have belief reaffirmed in the experience of worship on a fairly regular basis, a certain weakening can set in."

But worship alone, he feels, can become sterile if not backed up by involvement in the world.

"If you have a worship experience and the emphasis is theology and that's all, it can very easily degenerate into a kind of pietism.

"To me the life of Jesus as portrayed in the Gospels is a wonderful example of how this [combining worship and work] is done. Christ's own intense encounters with God and with those he chose to build and carry on his community gave his life a wholeness, both in his own being and in his relationships with those around him—the whole community, not just the disciples."

Ideally, he feels, the worship-work concept starts in the family setting. The church's role is to enlarge on it, nurture it, and bring it to fruition.

Dr. Brouwer, who is a dedicated and highly respected ecumenist, also says, "Our dozens of different liturgies, ethical systems, and dogmas constitute a maze that the ecumenical movement simply cannot pass by. We need to do our theological work in order to find our way toward one liturgy, united but not uniform, of the whole people of God."

Like Dr. Brouwer, Dr. James I. McCord feels that a vital Christianity starts with worship through prayer. Dr. McCord served as president of the Princeton Theological Seminary for twenty-four years and now heads the Center of Theological Inquiry in Princeton, New Jersey.

He says, "The greatest thing that churches can do is worship, and the greatest thing that Christians can do is pray."

But how can churches foster prayer? People feel a great need to pray, especially in times of stress, Dr. McCord says. "The disciples pleaded 'Lord, teach us to pray,' and he responded with the Lord's Prayer. Prayer is a lifeline to God, and if you don't have a prayer line, you don't have a relationship with God."

Asked why, in a period of renewed interest in religion nation-wide, the mainline Protestant churches have experienced a flattening and in some cases even losses in membership and church attendance while Catholic and some more fundamentalist Protestant churches have shown gains, he said, "I think some mainline churches made a very grave mistake in becoming too political, in making politics rather than religion their central emphasis. Don't misunderstand me. I think the God of the Bible is the God of politics too, but you do that [engage in politics] only from the standpoint of your spiritual commitment."

In assessing some poll results from the United Kingdom which indicated a precipitous drop in attendance and adherence, Dr. McCord said, "Yes, but you'll note that the churches that were most 'trendy' lost the most."

And on the recent revival of interest in fundamentalist Christianity:

"I suppose the most visible symbol of it is Jerry Falwell [founder of the Moral Majority movement], but I don't think that is where the strength of the religious revival in America is. I think that it is in the deep, evangelical piety that has characterized Americans' religion from the very beginnings.

"It's like a subterranean stream that surfaces and resurfaces again and again from generation to generation. And it's surfacing now, just as the mainline churches have flattened out. But it makes one realize the deep evangelistic spirituality of the American people."

On the fellowship aspect of Christianity, as exemplified by small worship and Bible-study groups and self-help organizations such as Alcoholics Anonymous:

"Remember the Apostles' Creed? It calls for 'the communion of saints,' and that is the explanation of what the church is. It is the community, the fellowship of believers. That is as close as you can come to what the Apostles' Creed calls the church."

How about the unchurched who have become "churched"? Why were they drawn to a congregation? Our polls show that an astounding 60 percent replied because they were *invited* by relatives or friends to participate. The polls offered ten other possible responses, but none got more than 8 percent. How can this response be accounted for? And what can Christians learn from it?

Dr. McCord replied, "Invitations show people that someone cares. That's important." He suggested a congregation be divided up into districts, with one or more lay persons responsible for each district. They could call on people and be prepared to offer spiritual counseling. "And we sometimes forget," he said, "that often the best spiritual counseling consists of just listening. Think of how many people pay fifty dollars an hour to a psychiatrist just for listening."

A spirited defense of historic Protestantism was offered by Rev. Gregory E. Reynolds, pastor of the Orthodox Presbyterian Church of New Rochelle, New York. He had been an architecture student and a member of the baby boom and Woodstock generations before he began studies for the ministry.

After experimenting with various life-styles and philosophies, he lived for a summer in a commune in Oregon.

"That did it. Suddenly I didn't have all the answers. I came face to face with an enemy I had never fully reckoned with: *sin.* Political revolution, psychedelic experience, and talk of peace and love were no match for it.

"When the phrase 'the teachings of Jesus' is used, most people believe that a courteous person is one who follows those teachings. . . . But he claimed to be God Incarnate—like no other man —the Messiah. So, more than just an ethical teacher, he was the Divine Creator-Redeemer. His ethical teachings penetrate far below the surface and unveil the depths of sin in the most courteous and kindly of people. . . . This simply accentuates a fact that we each wish to avoid—that we are sinners in need of more than a great teacher and example. We need a redeemer, a savior, and a lord.

"I don't always like the self-righteous way that some funda-

mentalists state what they believe. But I will defend their right
to say it. . . . Furthermore, I'm not ashamed to say I believe the
same Bible the fundamentalists believe. It is God's infallible
word. But the church needs to return to its Reformation roots.
As a nation we are in desperate need of the Bible's precepts, its
gospel, and its God."

Rev. Harris Hammond is a U.S. postal worker by day and
minister of the United Pentecostal Church of Havre, Montana,
on evenings and weekends. His small, ultrafundamentalist
church stands almost literally in the shadow of the steeples of two
of the major congregations in his town of some 13,000 population. On Sunday mornings the proximity to the Lutheran and
Catholic churches often causes parking problems and traffic jams.

But to him and his congregation of about forty members,
religion is the focus of their lives. "I see some revival of interest
in religion here," he said, "but this has always been a churchgoing town. A lot of it, though, is more social than religious, and
churchgoing and related activities are often more like coffee
klatches than services."

His flock sees some other denominations geared to surface
relationships with God and not always germane to worship and
an understanding of God's will.

Asked about the effects of various fundamentalist television
ministries on his congregation, he said that he had urged his flock
to ban television from their homes, mostly because of the emphasis on sex and violence shown. He himself does not own a television set and is confident that most of the members rarely watch
it.

For more than thirty years Father William Nolan has been
director of Aquinas House, a center for Catholic students who
attend Dartmouth College in Hanover, New Hampshire.

He has seen many student generations come and go and agrees
fully with the poll data that show a heightened interest in religious and moral values among today's college students, both as
spiritual experiences and as academic subjects.

"The 1960s and early 1970s were the tough years here [at
Dartmouth] and elsewhere," he said. "The turmoil of the Vietnam era was a big factor. By the mid-1970s or so things began

to get better. God often brings good out of evil, good out of heartache. The Vietnam affair shook young people up and they began to look for eternal values."

The serious search for these eternal values seemed to begin to grow in the mid-1970s—both among Catholics and Protestants, he said. "In fact, the Christian Fellowship movement and other fundamentalist movements among our Protestant brethren seemed to have sparked Catholic students into a deeper interest and commitment to their faith," he said.

The students' interest also developed its own flavor, both at Aquinas House and in the college's classrooms. Vatican II had allowed new forms of liturgy, including folk masses. He, personally, was not all that enthused about it when a group of some twenty-five student musicians asked to perform during services.

"Flutes, oboes, guitars, you name it. And you know, they were *good.* I'll bet we could tape-record them and get a best-selling record."

While he confessed that the folk mass wasn't his particular cup of tea at first, the service began to draw standing-room-only crowds. "And about a third of them were Protestants."

"It isn't so much a matter of converting anyone to Catholicism; it's a situation in which we could all join together in worship and honor God."

"Some of the Vatican Two changes—such as the music change —appeal greatly to the kids. Now, if we can get any change that gets them to look more deeply at eternal values, it's a definite plus."

(It might be noted, parenthetically, that Father Nolan is credited with influencing a significant number of students to go on and study for the priesthood after their time at Dartmouth, a nondenominational, highly selective Ivy League school.)

Rev. Shannon Bernard is minister of the Community Unitarian Church of White Plains, New York. She had served as an assistant minister of a Unitarian church in Berkeley, California, and as minister of a church in Orange, New Jersey. She holds master's degrees in psychology and divinity.

She began our interview by pointing out that most Unitarians are not Christians in the strictest sense. Most are theists, believing in one God but not necessarily the Holy Trinity. They accept the historical Jesus as an inspired teacher of ethics and morals but question his divinity. However, the church is remarkably free of dogmas, and members are encouraged to explore their own paths to an understanding of God and the human condition.

She was asked, "What do you think churches, especially the Unitarian Church, perhaps, can and should do to further spiritual as well as moral and ethical values?"

"We can provide a spiritual home for many people," she replied. "We deal with a good many 'comer-outers,' those from other religious backgrounds. Traditionally, our congregations are composed of about one third former Protestants, one third former Roman Catholics, and one third Jews.

"No one has all the answers or the whole truth. We are seeking life's essentials by being, doing, and becoming."

Unitarians proselytize, but in a "very low key" manner, she said. New members often come from interfaith marriages. "Often neither partner is willing to raise children in the faith of the other. For them the question is where can they find religious education programs for their children and a service for themselves that will not be anti-Protestant, anti-Catholic, or anti-Jewish but will find values in all creeds?"

Another source of new members is the group of Americans who feel that their church's teachings are more restrictive than they are willing to accept. However, they may feel a need to understand the purpose of their lives and even God's will for them.

On the division between worship and work, she says, "Unitarians probably come down on the side of work. We are traditionally very active in social concerns and charities, and individuals tend to worship in their own ways. In fact, there is an old joke which says that Unitarians address prayers 'To whom it may concern.' "

George Schonewald takes a slightly different tack in addressing what he feels churches and concerned laity could and should do. He is an intensely concerned Christian layman who feels strongly that "work," especially among the poor and needy, enhances the spiritual development of the "worker" and makes his or her worship all the more meaningful.

He points out that until the era of big government, Christian churches were the primary source of help for the needy and disadvantaged. Gradually government social programs took over, and as they grew larger they became less effective and more impersonal and bureaucratic.

Churches, he contends, should reemphasize their mission of aiding the poor. They should look beyond church fairs, women's guilds, and men's clubs—as useful as they are in fostering fellowship within a congregation—and reach out more positively to address the problems of the needy in a more involved, personal way.

Most churches have untapped human resources, lay people with expertise, time, and a willingness to become involved in worthy Christian causes, he says. Often they are just waiting to be asked. Church leaders could marshal these energies and put them to use in new and creative ways.

He acknowledges that many churches are already structured to do so, but argues that the needs and opportunities change constantly.

As just one example of the many helping services that a congregation might provide, he suggested a youth employment center. Unemployment, particularly among disadvantaged and minority youths, is a pressing and well-documented social problem. Interested church members, preferably with an interest in personnel work and counseling and a knowledge of job markets, could provide a clearinghouse for jobs and youthful job seekers that the congregation might identify. And given the disparity between the more affluent and less affluent congregations in many areas, there well could be an exchange of job information between churches.

"Helping the unemployed and underemployed would give individuals a welcome outlet for their desires to serve the Lord that they might not have found in the usual church activities. Their personal sense of satisfaction would be enriched almost as much as those they helped."

The authors had few doubts about the validity of their data but, like a reluctant surgical patient, sought a "second opinion," not only about the surveys' results but also about their interpretations. Dr. William C. McCready is program director of the National Opinion Research Center of the University of Chicago, which has done considerable opinion sampling on religious matters. He said that the center's data agreed substantially with the Gallup studies in most respects.

The NORC's surveys show that (1) Americans' Christian identification remains strong, (2) that there is a renewed interest in religion among virtually all elements of American society, (3) that religious images, such as those involving God, Jesus, and Mary, have a strong hold even on those with no religious training, and (4) that while some organized religions have lost adherents, those churchgoers who remain are reaching beyond the minimum requirements of their faith to investigate its deeper meanings and this has become their central religious experience.

Many are rejecting unquestioning obedience to religious authority and absolute moral guidelines. They have been imbued with many American ideas of freedom and the place of individual conscience.

"The transition is not from authority to anarchy but to conscience, and that's an uncomfortable, messy transition for many," he said.

But doesn't "going it alone" spiritually deprive one of the reinforcement and sense of community that churchgoing fosters? And what can concerned clergy and lay persons do? Where are they failing—if indeed they are?

Dr. McCready feels that if churches want to keep their traditions alive and thriving they should tie in more closely with modern culture that their congregations can relate to in order to transmit Christ's message.

He noted that Jesus' primary teaching tool was the parable. In using simple, vivid stories about everyday life that his listeners —mostly simple farmers and fishermen—could understand, he touched them in ways that deep theological discussions could not.

More Americans tend to think of their religious faith more in "mythic, imaginative, and reflective terms" than in standards of behavior. The need is to adapt without surrendering the basic teachings of Jesus. "He has been, after all, a conscience of the Western world for many centuries," Dr. McCready said.

Not everyone agrees that changes in liturgy and practice are necessary or even desirable. Some complain that such changes make them feel as if they are strangers in their own churches. Guitars instead of organ music? Sermons based on current social or political issues rather than the teachings of the Bible? Rock music instead of plainsong? And, for Catholics, the switch from services in Latin to the English language?

These were jarring experiences for many Christians.

Few, however, have expressed their misgivings and yearning for a "back-to-basics" philosophy as forcefully and as well as Malcolm Muggeridge, the outspoken British newspaper and magazine columnist and television personality. In late middle age, while filming a TV documentary in the Holy Land, he turned from a cynical, disbelieving curmudgeon into an articulate champion of Jesus and his message.

But what did he think churches could and should do? In an interview reprinted in his book *Jesus Rediscovered,* he pinpointed some of the dilemmas that clergy and concerned Christians face even today.

"I think the church, like most institutions in our society, is scared and is trying to ingratiate itself with people rather than to tell them the truth. Therefore, it takes an extremely equivocal attitude towards many of the moral issues that arise."

He was asked why the clergy often appear unenthusiastic for the things that they may believe. Isn't it difficult these days to convince people that there are any ultimate values?

"I shouldn't blame them [clergy] at all if they threw in their hand and said, 'I've had a go at this and it just can't be done, and I'm looking for another job.' I feel the utmost sympathy for them; but if you ask why the church is so weak—obviously an institution is weak if its aims bear little or no relation to the aims and teachings of its ministers."

And what should those aims be?

"The Gospel, the Christian Gospel; to teach people what Christ taught; to show them how he wanted them to live; how to love God and love their fellows."

Supposing nobody came to the church where that was done?

"It's perfectly understandable if a clergyman says, 'Nobody comes and I can't go on,' but what I think is absolutely fatal is not to say that, and instead to say, 'Let's make an adjustment, and see if we can't conform what we are preaching to what the mass-communications media are recommending.' There can be no adjustment; they are opposite things. Therein lies the dilemma and the fate of the church, I am afraid."

Dr. Paul E. Toms is pastor of the Park Street Church, an independent Congregational church in the heart of downtown Boston, Massachusetts. He is considered one of the nation's leading evangelical ministers in a large city with traditions of independent thought that is the home of many distinguished colleges and universities. In this intellectual hotbed, what special programs of education and outreach does his church provide?

"First, we like to think that we have a strong and biblically centered pulpit. In my own ministry and through invited speakers, we strive to suggest answers. People today are really searching deeply for some significant ideas of what their lives are all about. Families are concerned about the deterioration of family life; parents are concerned for their children and for the nation in terms of an apparent slippage of moral values. But they are also saying, What does all this mean in terms of myself, my own spiritual values?"

His church builds its approach to trying to win people to the Christian gospel through invitation and attraction.

"People respond more to invitation than to any other means. . . . This is not to denigrate the effectiveness of preaching, public meetings, individual readings of the Bible or literature. But your statistics [data from the polls] and our own experience clearly show that more people get their start in the Christian faith or their awareness of it through the intervention of others than in any other way."

Dr. Toms doesn't see a great Christian revival movement sweeping across the country, but he does sense a greater sensitivity and awareness of the need for a more personal relationship with God. Billy Graham was warmly received in New England communities and on campuses, and his meetings had a positive effect that is still being felt.

"But Christian churches must continue to reach out in compassion and understanding and clarity and back up their outreach by living a Christian life in such a way that people outside the church can see that it makes a difference. That's one of our great barriers. Some can say, 'I don't see any difference between you and the rest of us.'"

Dr. Toms has tailored his ministry to the specific needs of his large, sophisticated congregation, with several special Bible-centered programs that supplement his church's regular services. They include:

1. A strong college and university program. "We reach out to students and are represented on all the major campuses in this education-oriented city. Several hundred college students are regular participants in our services, and we have an associate minister for students and a student house."

2. A ministry aimed at young adults. Tens of thousands of professional and semiprofessional young people live in Boston and its suburbs and are involved in high technology, finance, and commerce. A special staff at the Park Street Church ministers to their spiritual needs.

3. Boston is also a center for "internationals," thousands of whom now live in the area with their families and are involved in education, business, and industry. His church conducts special classes for them in such things as English as a second language and American customs and Christian beliefs.

4. A strong missionary tradition exists among New England Protestant churches. Historically, they have supported missionaries in other sections of America and around the globe. The Park Street Church now supports some eighty such missionaries, and these efforts have not only spread the gospel but also given members a sense of active participation in its outreach.

Told that the polls showed that praying by oneself was the most-often mentioned method of worship, he said, "As a churchman I can understand that, but by the same token I have great appreciation of the gathering together of the people of God in a formal way, periodically or systematically, in the biblical pattern. I think that this can sometimes be deadening—there's no question about that, and we have to be very cautious about it. But where the institution is kept alive by the vibrant presence of God and the interaction of his people with his Spirit and his Word, it can be a very valuable experience."

Dean Anderson is an advertising executive, a born-again Christian, and an active member of the Reformed Presbyterian Church in Greenville, South Carolina.

His spiritual odyssey, from an unbaptized nonchurchgoer, to

church member and lay leader, and finally as a deeply committed Christian, provides a kind of case history of how involvement with Christians can deepen and even transform faith.

It began when he was about to be married. The minister required a baptismal certificate. Told by his mother that he had never been baptized, he went through the required rites. Later, after a period in the armed forces, he accepted a job in Greenville, but had to leave his family in Louisville, Kentucky, while he scouted for new quarters. To kill the lonely time away from his family, he began attending a nearby church on Sundays. It would be a good way, he reasoned, to get to know the people and the community better.

In a few short years, he found himself caught up in church activities as a Sunday school teacher and as a member of the church's board. His organizing and leadership talents led to his being appointed to arrange various training sessions for an evangelistic crusade that was scheduled in Greenville.

The pre-crusade training was instructive, but "it didn't get through to me," he says. "After all, I was already a baptized Christian; I believed in Christ and that he had been crucified and risen from the dead. How did the instructions and the message apply to me?"

The evangelist's message was powerful and effective, he says, but was not effectively followed up. Later, since he was co-chairman of the church's Commission on Evangelism, a friend suggested that a Lay Witness Evangelism program be arranged, and he agreed.

Lay persons from outside Greenville were brought in to share their salvation testimonies. "As I listened to them," he says, "I realized that they had had a personal relationship with Christ in their lives that I hadn't. What it was exactly escaped me at first, but in thinking about it I finally saw myself as a sinner for whom Christ had died."

At the concluding meeting, when the invitation was given, he walked quickly up the aisle, fell on his knees, and asked God "to come into my heart, change me, and make me like them."

In John 3, Jesus said, "except ye be born again, ye cannot see the kingdom of God," he noted. Looking back, he feels with certainty that only on that Sunday in March 1975 did he become a true Christian, born again by faith . . . a gift of God's grace.

7

Where Do We Go
from Here?
by George Gallup, Jr.

Whoever listens to the word but does not put it into
practice is like a man who looks in a mirror and sees
himself as he is. He takes a good look at himself and
then goes away and at once forgets what he looks like.
—James 1:23–24

Assuming that the critical issue in the church today is, as always, what we believe about Jesus Christ, what conclusions can
be drawn from this survey of late-twentieth-century America's
understanding of Jesus and commitment to him?

Certainly societal trends point to the fact that Americans have
not turned to Jesus Christ in any widespread or profound way.
A huge (81 percent) majority consider themselves Christians, yet
we permit hunger and poverty to exist on a widespread scale in
our land of abundance. We claim to be followers of Jesus Christ,
but we have stood idly by while some Americans have slipped
into something approaching a state of despair. An earlier survey
conducted for the Robert H. Schuller Ministries revealed that as
many as one third of our fellow citizens have a low sense of
self-worth, considered by many to be the number-one psychological problem in our society today.

We boast Christianity as our faith, but many of us have not
bothered to learn the basic biblical facts about this religion. Many
of us dutifully attend church, but this act in itself appears to have
made us no less likely than our unchurched brethren to engage
in unethical behavior.

We say we are Christians, but sometimes we do not show much
love toward those who do not share our particular religious
perspective. We say we rejoice in the good news that Jesus

brought, but we are often strangely reluctant to share the gospel with others. In a typical day the average person stays in front of the TV set nearly 25 times longer than in prayer.

We say we are *believers,* but perhaps we are only *assenters.*

Columnist Michael McManus questions the impact of religion in our society and makes this observation: "If religion does not produce a more ethical, loving society, something is fundamentally wrong with the way that religion is being practiced."

The paradox of high religious involvement and low ethics points to the pressing need to reexamine the usual approaches to deepening the spiritual commitment of Americans. The results of this discussion of America's response to Jesus Christ call, we believe, for action.

As we turn to additional steps that churches might consider, we note findings from a number of Gallup surveys suggesting that the prospect for deepening America's spiritual commitment is far from hopeless. Virtually all Americans are, in some measure, drawn to the person of Jesus Christ. We saw that. Many believe he is the Son of God, and even many among the nondevout feel that Jesus' life and person tell us something profound about the meaning of existence. And, remarkably, as many as 9 in 10 say that Jesus as a moral and ethical leader has had at least some impact upon their lives.

Furthermore, at least half of Americans wish their religious faith were stronger, and a perhaps surprising one fifth of nonbelievers say they would *like* to believe in the divinity of Jesus Christ.

A majority of Americans believe in a "living Christ" and many find his presence in nature, in times of personal crisis, in the lives of other Christians, and when they spend time with people in need. "What is unique about Jesus," wrote Malcolm Muggeridge, "is that, on the testimony and in the experience of innumerable people, of all sorts and conditions, of all races and nationalities, from the simplest and the most primitive to the most sophisticated and cultivated, he remains alive."

A remarkable 4 in 10 Americans have an intuitive or experiential basis for their belief and report a dramatic religious experience—a turning point in their lives when they committed themselves to Jesus Christ. And 7 in 10 of all survey respondents feel that their relationship with Jesus Christ is deepening.

As many as 8 in 10 Americans, in addition, believe God has
a plan for their lives, and no fewer than 7 in 10 say it is either
"completely" or "mostly" true that they "constantly seek God's
will through prayer."

And, finally, the vast majority of Christians readily admit that
they do not come very close to following the example of Jesus.
And similarly high numbers admit they have failed to make an
all-out effort to follow the example of Jesus.

One cannot reflect upon these figures and fail to see the great
potential for deepening spiritual commitment among Americans.
The findings suggest that lack of commitment is not so much a
question of carefully considered nonbelief as it is a matter of
sidestepping or running away from the issue of Jesus Christ in
one's life. John R. W. Stott, in *Basic Christianity,* wrote:

> An appreciable number of people throughout the world are still
> brought up in Christian homes in which the truth of Christ and of
> Christianity is assumed. But when their critical faculties develop
> and they begin to think for themselves, they find it easier to
> discard the religion of their childhood than make the effort to
> investigate its credentials.

What steps seem indicated if we are to deepen the spiritual
commitment of Americans? Here is a general approach that
might be considered by a clergy person starting out with a new
parish.

First, recognize the thirst for the "living" Christ among
Americans and the desire for a stronger faith, as the survey
clearly reveals.

Next, collect basic information (through surveys and other
means) about a given church and the people it is to serve. To
know where we are going, we must first find out where we are
today; to do otherwise is to grope blindly toward the future.
Carefully designed surveys can help answer basic questions about
levels of belief and commitment and aid in the effort to maintain
a healthy balance of evangelism, social concern, and spiritual
renewal.

Now it's all very well to have a mass of statistics and a set of
priorities, but it's another matter to get support for your plan of
action. After all, clergy are dealing not only with unbelief but
with lethargy and fear of commitment, as well as the many activi-

ties competing for people's time. How does one attempt to dispel this lethargy and encourage greater commitment to a course of action?

One step that might be considered, discussed earlier, is to encourage participation in small-group fellowship, which (in addition to private prayer and corporate worship) could be considered the missing third dimension in people's spiritual lives today. The formation of such cell groups under the aegis of a central church could strengthen commitment to a church.

Second, encourage worship on a daily basis, either in a small group or a church. In view of the distractions of modern life and the lack of self-discipline in people's lives, churches would do well to encourage their flock to make a commitment to worship on a regular, preferably daily, basis, either in church or in a small fellowship or prayer group. Once-a-week (usually Sunday) worship may not provide enough spiritual nourishment for Christians who wish to mature in their faith. Harvey Cox has written that "the failure of most churches to teach people how to pray, and the difficulties involved in learning the difference between reading, studying, and meditation on a text, have produced a generation of Protestants who have practically no spiritual discipline at all."

A third way to change lukewarm involvement into deep commitment is to encourage people to challenge their faith. People should be encouraged not only to answer the question of Jesus in their lives—"to examine the credentials of Christianity," as Stott puts it—but also to question their own beliefs. Furthermore, persons should be encouraged to question seriously the assumption that their own denomination is the one in which their faith can best be nurtured.

Paul Little reminds us that we must know *why* we believe: "We live in an increasingly sophisticated and educated world. It is no longer enough to know *what* we believe. It is essential to know *why* we believe it. Believing something doesn't make it true." Such hard questions can only result in a strengthened faith. Surely, the strongest Christians are the challenged Christians.

Episcopal bishop John Selby Spong in *The Easter Moment* writes:

I am convinced that the only authentic defense of the faith involves honest scholarship, not anti-intellectual hiding from truth. There is a sense in which our scholarship ought to be so deep, so honest, and so intensive that the result will be either that what we believe will crumble before our eyes, incapable of being sustained, or that we will discover a power and a reality so true that our commitment will be total. If we do not risk the former, we will never discover the latter. Nothing less than this seems worthy of Christians.

A fourth way to energize the people of your church is to consider developing programs that bring them face to face with the needy. Many Christians in our nation, it is probably safe to say, have never had a meaningful one-on-one experience with persons in dire need. Yet without this kind of exposure, it is often difficult for a person to generate the kind of dedication needed to try to improve the lot of the poor, certainly a basic requirement of a Christian. What is called for is a kind of crisis intervention on a broad scale, with "high self-esteem" people meeting and working directly with "low self-esteem" people. The first step is caring in a deep way. If we truly care about the plight of others, we will do something. We will be impelled to action.

We have to do more than spend money. Thoreau once said, "If you give money, spend yourself with it." If those who serve on boards or committees dealing with human needs, for example, matched every hour spent sitting in the boardroom with an hour of direct face-to-face involvement with the less fortunate, society would feel the impact and our committee work would be given new life.

In the last analysis, in our efforts to encourage greater commitment, we come to prayer. Nothing will happen until people have developed their prayer life to the extent that it becomes a cherished moment in their daily routine when they gain a renewed sense of partnership with God. Deepened prayer lives will lead to living a more sincere Christian life, described so simply but powerfully by Eric Liddell (whose life was portrayed in *Chariots of Fire*) in a book on his life, *The Disciplines of the Christian Life:*

As Christians, I challenge you. Have a great aim—have high standards—make Jesus your ideal. Be like him in character. Be like him in outlook and attitude toward God and others. Be like him in the home—thoughtful, patient, loving. Be like him in your work—honest, reliable, always willing to go the second mile. Be like him in your social life—approachable, unselfish, considerate. Make him an ideal not merely to be admired but also to be followed.

We need also to be reminded of the deeper rewards of a sincere faith—and to bear in mind Jesus' words: "Ask, and you will receive; seek, and you will find; knock, and the door will be opened to you" (Matt. 7:7).

In view of Jesus' words, it is interesting to note from the survey (although a direct cause-and-effect relationship cannot, of course, be established) that of those who say they have made the "greatest possible effort" to follow Jesus' example, 8 in 10 say their relationship with Jesus increases their sense of self-worth "a great deal."

One often senses the rewards, or the fruits of faith, when in the presence of others. In the survey, for example, 3 in 10 said they could tell whether a person is a sincere Christian even after only a brief encounter. (See Table 34.) In a message at the Leadership Luncheon following the 1983 National Prayer Breakfast in Washington, John Stott said:

> When we meet some people we know immediately and instinctively that they are different. We are anxious to learn their secret. It is not the way they dress or talk or behave, although it influences these things. It is not that they have affixed a name tag to themselves and proclaimed themselves the adherent of a particular religion or ideology. It's not even that they have a strict moral code which they faithfully follow. It is that they know Jesus Christ, and that he is a living reality to them. They dwell in him and he dwells in them. He is the source of their life and it shows in everything they do.
>
> These people have an inner serenity which adversity cannot disturb; it is the peace of Christ. They have a spiritual power that physical weakness cannot destroy; it is the power of Christ. They have a hidden vitality that even the process of dying and death cannot quelch; it is the life of Christ.

As the two thousandth anniversary of Christ's birth approaches, are Americans coming any closer to a commitment to truly love one another, as Christ commanded? By way of answer, one is tempted to quote C. C. Colton: "Men will wrangle for religion; write for it; fight for it; die for it; anything but—live for it."

And Jonathan Swift: "We have just enough religion to make us hate. But not enough to make us love one another."

And yet, in the 1980s, we are seeing new signs of spiritual hunger and a thirst for the living Christ—reflected in a growth in Bible study and prayer fellowship groups, reinforced by new religious ferment on the college campuses of the nation, and capped by the finding that as many as 7 in 10 Americans believe their relationship with Jesus is deepening (Table 35).

The goal, a Christian would acknowledge, is to surrender our lives to God's control and let the love of Christ operate in our hearts. Looked at in interfaith and interdenominational terms, this means reaching out not only to those most reachable— persons in the same religious tradition—but also to those at the other end of the religious spectrum. Surely one of the saddest developments in contemporary Christianity is the gap in under- standing and sympathy between Christians in the conservative and liberal traditions.

Mark J. Galli, pastor of Grace Presbyterian Church in Sac- ramento, California, writes in an article in *Christianity Today,* "Living with Those Who Disagree" (July 12, 1985, p. 60):

> *Finally, remember what the church is.* A true church is marked by both biblical doctrine and biblical love. Of course we must hold to the Bible's teaching about God. But orthodoxy in doctrine is not to be joined to heterodoxy in ethics. We please God when we believe his standards of truth—and obey his standards of conduct based on that truth. If we fail to love one another, our theology turns to ashes. I cannot hope to keep everyone happy, but I can keep from alienating people because of my insensitivity.

A recent survey conducted by The Gallup Organization for the Robert H. Schuller Ministries on religious prejudice shows sharp differences between religious conservatives and liberals in religious beliefs and on other matters, but also significant areas of agreement that could become the basis for ministries aimed at achieving greater unity between the two wings of Christian- ity. The survey pointed to a commonality in views on issues, in goals, in the outlook for Christianity in the United States, as well as commonalities in basic beliefs and in religious interests.

The most important part of Jesus' mission, in the view of survey respondents, was to "show us how to really love one another." Surely the truest mark of Christians is love for one another. Jesus said, "And now I give you a new commandment: love one another. As I have loved you, so you must love one another. If you have love for one another, then everyone will know that you are my disciples" (John 13:34–35).

Where there is love, miracles can happen.

Afterword
by Robert H. Schuller

The two Georges, Gallup and O'Connell, have succeeded admirably, I think, in analyzing and making sense out of the mountains of computer printouts and other data collected over several years.

Generally, I'm uncomfortable with statistics. I prefer dealing with people and ideas; I'm more responsive to intuitions and feelings than to numbers. But I know that we all can learn much from poll results that are scientifically gathered and intelligently interpreted.

Better still, they have fleshed out the data with what they call the "voices," the verbalized views of representative Americans about their perceptions of Jesus and some thoughts of clergy and other concerned Christians about how to attract nonbelievers and waverers to heed Jesus' message.

As those who have heard my sermons at the Crystal Cathedral or in my *Hour of Power* telecasts know all too well, I firmly believe in a positive attitude toward life. I am convinced that one *cannot* love God and neighbor unless one first loves oneself. And loving oneself vastly increases the chances that one will be able to know, love, and serve God and neighbor.

From time to time in recent years, I have suggested and argued for a "New Reformation." The original Christian Reformation in the sixteenth century, of course, brought about substantial changes in the ways that Christians worship. And, in retrospect, I think we can say that the Reformation and the Counter-Reformation that followed purified and strengthened both the Reformers and the previously dominant Roman Catholic churches.

Perhaps it is too early to say that a new crisis exists in the Christian community today, but polls and other evidence suggest that many Americans are not being served adequately by their churches even as surveys suggest that the interest in spiritual values has increased.

The right "chemistry" is a modern buzzword. In interpersonal relationships this term implies that business associates, husbands and wives, even parents and children be essentially in agreement on ends and means. But chemistry involves catalysts, substances that aid or speed up reactions between compounds while remaining unchanged themselves.

I often think that churches were intended to be catalysts, to teach and bring God and humankind closer together. The analogy breaks down a bit, however, because churches should be able to change too as they mediate.

A newspaper interviewer once asked me how I would like to be remembered here on earth. After thinking about it for a moment, I replied, "I would like to be remembered as someone who inspired, who ignited a spark of hope where there had been discouragement. If I ignite a spark of hope, probably I have produced the possibility of faith, and then love becomes a possibility. Finally, in the presence of hope, miracles happen."

We cannot predict that miracles will result from the publication of this book. We do hope it suggests some possibilities and insights that will benefit the Christian community.

Appendix

1. Did Christ Live? Was He God?

The questions: *Do you believe that Jesus Christ ever actually lived? Do you think he was God, or just another religious leader like Mohammed or Buddha?* (Asked of those responding *Yes, Christ lived.*)

	All Respondents	Relation with Jesus Increases Self-worth Great Deal	Greatest Effort to Follow Jesus' Example	Religion Very Important
Yes, Christ lived	91%	98%	100%	96%
Christ was God	70	87	90	82
Just religious leader	11	4	2	5
Other	6	5	4	6
Don't know	4	2	4	3
No, Christ did not live	2	1	*	1
Don't know	7	1	*	3
Total	100%	100%	100%	100%

*Less than one half of one percent

2. Desire to Believe in the Divinity of Jesus

The question: *Do you wish you could believe in the divinity of Jesus, or does it not make a great deal of difference to you?* (Asked of those who believe Christ lived but was not God.)

Wish could believe	20%
Not make a great deal of difference	44
No opinion	36
Total	100%

3. Beliefs About Jesus

The question: *Which one of these statements comes closest to describing your beliefs about Jesus?*

	All Respondents	Relation with Jesus Increases Self-worth Great Deal	Greatest Effort to Follow Jesus' Example	Religion Very Important
Jesus was divine in the sense that he was in fact God living among men	42%	53%	63%	52%
Jesus was divine in the sense that while he was only a man, he was uniquely called by God to reveal God's purpose in the world	27	29	21	28
Jesus was divine in the sense that he embodied the best that is in all men	9	9	6	7
Jesus was a great man and teacher, but I could not call him divine	6	2	4	3
Frankly, I'm not entirely sure there really was such a person	2	*	*	*
No opinion	14	7	6	10
Total	100%	100%	100%	100%

*Less than one half of one percent

4. Importance of Belief That Christ Was Fully God and Fully Human

The question: *In your own life, how important is this belief to you?*

	Very Important	Fairly Important	Not Very Important	Not Important	No Opinion
General Public	58%	23%	9%	8%	2%
Religious Ideology					
Conservatives	82	13	2	2	1
Moderates	63	26	7	3	1
Liberals	40	27	15	17	1
Evangelicals					
Evangelicals	92	6	1	1	*
Non-evangelicals	49	28	11	9	3
Level of Self-Esteem					
Very high	62	21	7	10	*
Other	55	25	10	6	4
Effort to Understand					
Great deal/some	69	20	5	5	1
Hardly any/none	48	28	13	9	2
Great Deal of Contact With					
Conservatives	77	15	3	4	1
Liberals	67	19	6	8	*
Religious Preference					
Protestants	67	21	7	3	2
Catholics	58	29	5	4	4
Protestant Denomination					
All Baptists	72	19	6	3	*
Southern Baptists	81	15	2	2	*
Methodists	61	27	8	4	*
Sex					
Men	50	27	12	9	2
Women	66	20	5	6	3
Age					
18–29 years old	53	27	11	7	2
30–49 years old	55	25	10	8	2
50 and older	66	19	5	7	3

*Less than one percent

5. Doubts About Jesus' Return to Earth

The question: *According to the Bible, Jesus promised to return to earth someday. Do you have serious doubts that this will happen, have some doubts that this will happen, or have no doubts that this will happen?*

	All Respondents	Jesus Was God	Relation with Jesus Increases Self-worth Great Deal	Greatest Effort to Follow Jesus' Example	Religion Very Important
Serious doubts	10%	3%	4%	5%	5%
Some doubts	16	11	8	6	9
No doubts	62	81	83	82	79
Has already happened or is happening (volunteered)	1	1	2	4	1
No opinion	11	4	3	3	6
Total	100%	100%	100%	100%	100%

6. Jesus' Most Appealing Character or Personality Traits

The question: *What do you consider to be the most appealing character or personality traits of Jesus?*

	All Respondents	Jesus Was God	Relation with Jesus Increases Self-worth Great Deal	Greatest Effort to Follow Jesus' Example	Religion Very Important
Love for humankind	41%	53%	55%	54%	51%
Forgiveness	13	15	16	16	14
Kindness	9	11	10	10	10
Compassion	7	10	10	12	9
Help/guidance	7	7	6	8	7
Humility	6	8	7	7	7
Knowledge/ understanding	6	8	6	5	6
Caring	6	7	6	6	7
Teachings	6	5	7	6	6
Promise of salvation	6	8	10	11	8
Everything about him is good	6	6	6	8	7
Honesty	5	6	6	5	5
Patience/calmness	3	3	2	2	3
Strength	3	4	5	3	3
Healing	3	3	6	7	4
Gentleness	2	2	3	2	2
Ethics	2	1	2	1	2
Divinity	2	2	3	2	3
Miracles	1	1	2	2	2
Hope	1	2	1	3	1
Miscellaneous	1	*	*	*	1
Don't know	20	9	8	8	13

*Less than one half of one percent.
NOTE: Totals add to more than 100 because of multiple response.

7. Word Picture of Jesus

The question: *For each pair of words on this card, tell me the number that comes closest to the way you would describe Jesus. For example, if you consider Jesus proud, say "1," and if you consider Jesus humble, say "7." If you consider Jesus between proud and humble, you might say "4."*

	All Respondents	Jesus Was God	Relation with Jesus Increases Self-worth Great Deal	Greatest Effort to Follow Jesus' Example	Religion Very Important
	Mean	Mean	Mean	Mean	Mean
Demanding = 1 Accepting = 7	5.3	5.2	5.6	6.0	5.5
Easy to understand = 1 Hard to understand = 7	2.8	2.6	2.4	2.1	2.6
Physically strong = 1 Physically weak = 7	2.2	2.0	1.9	1.9	2.0
Brave = 1 Cowardly = 7	1.5	1.4	1.4	1.4	1.4
Warm = 1 Aloof = 7	1.5	1.4	1.4	1.3	1.5
Fun-loving = 1 Somber = 7	3.7	3.6	3.4	3.4	3.5
Impractical = 1 Practical = 7	5.8	6.1	6.1	6.2	6.0
Physically attractive = 1 Physically unattractive = 7	2.6	2.6	2.2	2.3	2.5
Emotionally stable = 1 Emotionally unstable = 7	1.5	1.3	1.3	1.3	1.4
Strong personality = 1 Weak personality = 7	1.4	1.3	1.3	1.3	1.3
Without sin = 1 Sinful = 7	1.7	1.4	1.5	1.5	1.5
Imperfect = 1 Perfect = 7	6.1	6.4	6.4	6.6	6.3
Divine = 1 Human = 7	2.5	1.9	2.0	1.8	2.2

8. Public Pronouncements by Religious Organizations on
   Ethical-Moral Matters

   The question: *How important do you feel it is for religious organizations to make public statements about what they feel to be the will of God in ethical-moral matters? Would you say it is very important, fairly important, not very important, or not at all important?*

	Very Important	Fairly Important	Not Very Important	Not at All Important	No Opinion
General Public	36%	33%	14%	11%	6%
Sex					
Men	38	28	16	13	5
Women	34	38	13	9	6
Religious Preference					
Catholic	31	40	13	9	7
Protestant	41	33	14	8	4
Denomination					
Southern Baptist	60	27	4	6	3
Baptist	53	27	9	4	7
Methodist	29	44	18	7	2
Lutheran	30	35	25	8	2
Age					
18–29 years	24	40	17	13	6
30–49 years	40	30	14	11	5
50 and older	42	31	13	9	5
Education					
College background	31	33	19	13	4
High school	36	35	14	10	5
Grade school	48	27	9	8	8
Region					
East	31	38	14	11	6
Midwest	32	33	18	11	6
South	48	29	8	9	6
West	31	33	19	13	4

9. Religious Organizations That Work to Defeat Politicians

The question: *Certain religious groups are working actively for the defeat of political candidates who don't agree with their position on certain issues. Do you think they should or should not do this?*

	Should	Should Not	No Opinion
General Public	30%	52%	18%

10. Religious Organizations That Try to Persuade Politicians

The question: *Do you think religious organizations should or should not try to persuade Senators and Representatives to enact legislation they would like to see become law?*

	Should	Should Not	No Opinion
General Public	41%	45%	14%
Sex			
Men	39	48	13
Women	42	42	16
Religious Preference			
Catholic	44	42	14
Protestant	42	44	14
Denomination			
Southern Baptist	54	36	10
Baptist	49	33	18
Methodist	37	49	14
Lutheran	46	46	8
Age			
18–29 years	43	42	15
30–49 years	40	46	14
50 and older	39	46	15
Education			
College background	43	48	9
High school	39	45	16
Grade school	42	38	20
Region			
East	42	45	13
Midwest	39	45	16
South	44	40	16
West	34	53	13

11. Protestant Denominational Preference

The question: *What is your denomination?* (Asked of those who said they were Protestants.)

		Percent
Baptist churches		20
Southern Baptist Convention	9	
American Baptist Churches	2	
The National Baptist Convention of America	1	
The National Baptist Convention of U.S.A., Inc.	*	
Other Baptist	3	
Baptist, don't know which denomination	5	
Methodist churches		9
United Methodist Church	7	
A.M.E. Zion Church	*	
A.M.E. Church	*	
Other Methodist	1	
Methodist, don't know which denomination	1	
Lutheran churches		7
American Lutheran Church	2	
Lutheran Church in America	1	
Missouri Synod Lutheran	2	
Other Lutheran	1	
Lutheran, don't know which denomination	1	
Presbyterian churches		2
Episcopal churches		3
United Church of Christ (or Congregationalist or Evangelical and Reformed)		2
Other Protestant		2
Protestant unspecified		5
Other		7
Total		57

*Less than one percent
NOTE: In reading the tables, we should bear in mind that the respondents themselves designated their denominations. Therefore, Southern Baptists may be confused with Baptists who live in the South but do not belong to the Southern Baptist Convention, and it is likely that some survey respondents in the South and West who belong to the Church of Christ identified themselves with the *United* Church of Christ.

12. Religious Preference

The question: *What is your religious preference—Protestant, Roman Catholic, Jewish, or none?*

	Protestant	Catholic	Jewish	No Religious Preference
General Public	57%	28%	2%	9%
Sex				
Men	55	27	3	11
Women	59	28	2	6
Age				
18–24 years	52	30	2	12
25–29 years	50	30	2	13
30–49 years	56	28	3	9
50–64 years	62	28	3	4
65 and older	66	24	3	4
Region				
East	40	44	6	7
Midwest	63	26	1	7
South	74	16	1	7
West	48	26	2	13
Race				
Whites	55	30	3	8
Non-whites	72	14	*	9
Blacks	82	7	*	7
Hispanics	18	70	*	9
Education				
College graduates	53	26	6	11
Some college	55	28	3	9
High school graduates	59	29	2	6
Some high school	61	27	1	7
Politics				
Republicans	64	24	1	5
Democrats	56	30	4	7
Independents	55	28	2	11
Occupation				
Professional and business	53	28	4	9
Clerical and sales	56	29	2	9
Manual workers	57	29	1	8
Non-labor force	64	25	3	5
Income				
$40,000 and over	52	31	5	8
$30,000–$39,999	54	31	3	8
$20,000–$29,999	56	29	2	8
$10,000–$19,999	60	26	2	8
Under $10,000	62	24	1	8
Labor Union				
Labor union families	53	34	2	7
Non-labor union families	58	27	3	8

*Less than one percent

13. Impact of Jesus as a Moral and Ethical Teacher

The question: *What impact would you say Jesus, as a moral and ethical teacher, has had on your life?*

	Great Impact	Some	Hardly Any	None	No Opinion
General Public	61%	26%	4%	3%	6%
Sex					
Men	55	31	5	4	5
Women	67	22	3	3	5
Age					
18–24	41	43	6	5	5
25–29	57	32	3	3	5
30–49	62	25	4	3	6
50–64	67	20	2	2	9
65 or older	74	15	2	4	5
Marital Status					
Married	65	24	2	3	6
Single	44	41	5	6	4
Divorced/separated/widowed	67	16	6	3	8
Religiosity					
Jesus was God	79	18	1	1	1
Relation with Jesus greatly increases self-worth	88	10	1	*	1
Making greatest effort to follow Jesus' example	96	3	*	*	1
Religion very important	83	12	1	1	3

14. Self-estimation as Christian

The question: *Do you consider yourself to be a Christian?*

	Yes	No	Undecided
General Public	81%	12%	7%
Age			
18–24	78	17	5
25–29	76	13	11
30–49	80	14	6
50–64	84	7	16
65 or older	89	7	4
High Religiosity			
Jesus was God	93	5	2
Relation with Jesus greatly increases self-worth	96	3	1
Making greatest effort to follow Jesus' example	98	2	0
Religion very important	92	5	3
Low Religiosity			
Not church member	61	28	11
Jesus was not divine	50	47	3
Relation with Jesus increases self-worth little if at all	58	36	6
Little or no effort to follow Jesus' example	51	43	6
Religion not very important	45	39	16

15. Most Important Ways to Try to Follow Jesus

The question: *Of the statements on this card, which four do you think are the most important if someone is trying to be a follower of Jesus?*

	All Respond-ents	Jesus Was God	Relation with Jesus Increases Self-worth Great Deal	Greatest Effort to Follow Jesus' Example	Religion Very Import-ant
Obeying the Ten Commandments	48%	53%	52%	51%	51%
Forgiving those who have wronged you	44	50	48	40	46
Putting others' needs before your own	34	37	40	35	34
Living in such a way as to draw others to Jesus	31	40	42	43	38
Person-to-person charitable activities among the underprivileged, the sick, the elderly	23	20	20	21	22
Consoling those in sorrow or affliction	23	21	22	17	21
Telling people about Jesus	22	30	33	34	29
Being active in a local church	20	25	26	27	24
Studying the Bible daily	19	24	30	30	25
Having a regular prayer time	19	26	30	32	25
Counseling and praying with those who need support and encouragement	17	19	16	15	17
Being cheerful in every situation	17	19	18	21	18
Receiving Holy Communion	14	16	16	19	17
Becoming involved in community activities	10	8	7	7	9
Working for social justice	10	9	8	7	7
Don't know	14	4	3	4	8

NOTE: Totals add to more than 100 because of multiple responses.

16. Relative Importance of the First and Second Commandments

The question: *Which comes closer to how you feel?*

	All Respondents	Jesus Was God	Relation with Jesus Increases Self-worth Great Deal	Greatest Effort to Follow Jesus' Example	Religion Very Important
Love God and then your neighbor	64%	78%	83%	83%	80%
Love your neighbor and then God	11	6	3	3	4
Both equal (volunteered)	17	15	13	13	13
No opinion	8	1	1	1	3
Total	100%	100%	100%	100%	100%

17. Ways in Which Jesus Has Entered Respondents' Lives

The question: *In what ways, if any, is Jesus entering or has entered your life, or is having an effect on your life?*

	All Respond-ents	Jesus Was God	Relation with Jesus Increases Self-worth Great Deal	Greatest Effort to Follow Jesus' Example	Religion Very Import-ant
Helped or guided me	10%	12%	15%	16%	13%
Set an example for me to follow	9	11	12	12	10
Helped during illness/gave me health	8	9	10	15	10
Helped me have compassion	8	10	12	14	10
Improved my outlook and thinking	7	10	9	12	10
Helped me have peace and calmed me	6	7	9	8	8
His teachings have helped me be a better person	6	6	9	9	7
Blessed me with a good life/family	5	7	8	8	7
Helped me through my prayers	4	5	5	7	6
Saved me from sin/saved my soul	3	4	5	8	4
I feel better and happier	3	5	6	5	5
Gave me courage	3	3	5	4	4
Helped me accept death	3	4	3	4	3
He watches over me/cares for me	2	3	3	4	3
He shows me right from wrong	2	3	4	2	3
I now go to church	2	1	2	*	2
He comforts me	1	2	2	3	2
Helps me be patient	1	*	1	*	1
None	14	6	3	1	4
Miscellaneous	*	1	*	1	*
Don't know	22	16	11	9	16

*Less than one half of one percent.
NOTE: Totals add to more than 100 because of multiple responses.

18. Effort to Follow Jesus' Example

The question: *How hard have you tried to follow the example of Jesus—if at all?*

	Greatest Possible	Consider-able	Some	Hardly Any	None	No Opinion
General Public	12%	33%	34%	8%	5%	8%
Sex						
Men	9	27	38	11	6	9
Women	15	40	30	5	3	7
Age						
18–24 years	4	28	44	11	7	6
25–29 years	6	32	37	13	6	6
30–49 years	11	32	35	9	6	8
50–64 years	13	38	31	5	3	10
65 and older	28	36	23	3	2	8
Education						
College graduate	8	31	39	7	9	6
Some college	8	34	38	8	5	7
High school	11	33	35	9	4	7
Grade school	26	35	20	5	2	12
Race						
White	11	33	35	8	5	8
Nonwhite	24	33	26	6	3	8
Religious Preference						
Catholic	8	37	39	8	2	6
Protestant	17	37	34	6	1	5
Denomination						
Baptist	21	36	31	6	*	6
Southern Baptist	20	38	33	6	*	4
Methodist	12	31	44	6	1	6
Lutheran	11	40	38	5	2	4
Religiosity						
Jesus was God	19	41	32	5	1	2
Relation with Jesus greatly increases self-worth	27	49	22	2	*	*
Religion very important	21	44	27	3	1	4

*Less than one half of one percent

19. Closeness to Following Jesus' Example

The question: *How close do you feel you yourself come in following the example of Jesus?*

	All Respondents	Greatest Possible Effort	Considerable Effort	Some Effort	Hardly Any or No Effort
Very close	10%	44%	11%	4%	1%
Fairly close	47	47	67	49	16
Not very close	26	6	19	41	35
Not at all close	8	1	3	4	42
No opinion	9	2	*	2	6
Total	100%	100%	100%	100%	100%

*Less than one half of one percent

20. Involvement in Various Activities

The question: *How often, if at all, during the past year have you done each of the following?*

	Never	Once	Several Times	Many Times	Don't Know	Total
Supported the nuclear freeze movement in some way, such as signing a petition or attending a rally	87%	8%	4%	1%	*	100%
Donated time to help someone (other than a family member) who was sick or in need	29	13	44	13	1	100
Spent quiet times by yourself in prayer, meditation, or personal Bible study	27	7	39	27	*	100
Done volunteer work at your church, such as teaching, cleaning, or committee work	62	6	19	13	*	100
Done volunteer work for a community organization, other than a church, such as a civic group or charity	62	9	20	9	*	100

*Less than one half of one percent

21. Extent to Which Relationship with Jesus Increases Self-worth

The question: *To what extent, if at all, does your relationship with Jesus increase your sense of self-worth—that is, make you feel better about yourself?*

	All Respondents	Jesus Was God	Believe God Loves Them to a Great Extent	Greatest Effort to Follow Jesus' Example	Religion Very Important
A great deal	36%	46%	48%	78%	54%
Somewhat	37	42	38	15	34
Hardly at all	8	7	5	3	4
Not at all	8	2	3	1	2
No opinion	11	3	6	3	6
Total	100%	100%	100%	100%	100%

22. Sensing Jesus' Presence

The question: *Have you sensed Jesus' presence?*

	All Respondents	Jesus Was God	Relation with Jesus Increases Self-worth Great Deal	Greatest Effort to Follow Jesus' Example	Religion Very Important
In nature					
Often	43%	58%	68%	73%	60%
Sometimes	21	22	17	14	18
Occasionally	13	11	9	7	10
Never	13	7	5	2	7
No opinion	10	2	1	4	5
Total	100%	100%	100%	100%	100%
In times of personal crisis					
Often	46	60	76	85	66
Sometimes	25	26	17	9	21
Occasionally	8	6	4	2	4
Never	12	6	2	1	4
No opinion	9	2	1	3	5
Total	100%	100%	100%	100%	100%
In church or religious services					
Often	46	63	75	82	67
Sometimes	21	19	17	11	17
Occasionally	10	10	4	4	6
Never	13	6	3	2	5
No opinion	10	2	1	1	5
Total	100%	100%	100%	100%	100%

23. Occurrence of Born-again Experiences

The question: *Would you say that you have been born again or have had a born-again experience—that is, a turning point in your life when you committed yourself to Jesus Christ?*

	Yes	No	No Opinion
General Public	38%	53%	9%
Sex			
Men	32		
Women	43		
Age			
18–24 years	36		
25–29 years	35		
30–49 years	36		
50–64 years	38		
65 or older	45		
Education			
College graduate	25		
Some college	34		
High school	38		
Grade school	52		
Marital Status			
Married	40		
Single	30		
Race			
White	35		
Nonwhite	51		
Religious Preference			
Catholic	21		
Protestant	52		

24. Nature of Born-again Experiences

The question: *Was the born-again experience sudden, gradual, or both?*

	All Respondents	Jesus Was God	Relation with Jesus Increases Self-worth Great Deal	Greatest Effort to Follow Jesus' Example	Religion Very Important
Yes	38%	52%	65%	76%	55%
Sudden	8	11	16	18	12
Gradual	20	27	31	35	29
Both	10	14	18	23	14
No opinion	*	*	*	*	*
No	53	45	33	23	39
No opinion	9	3	2	1	6
Total	100%	100%	100%	100%	100%

*Less than one half of one percent

25. Knowledge of Jesus' Delivering the Sermon on the Mount

The question: *Who delivered the Sermon on the Mount?*

	All Respondents	Jesus Was God	Relation with Jesus Increases Self-worth Great Deal	Greatest Effort to Follow Jesus' Example	Religion Very Important
Jesus	42%	54%	53%	67%	51%
Incorrect answer	24	24	28	16	24
Don't know	34	22	19	17	25
Total	100%	100%	100%	100%	100%

26. Knowledge of the Four Gospels

The question: *Will you tell me the names of the first four books of the New Testament of the Bible—that is, the four Gospels?*

	All Respondents	Jesus Was God	Relation with Jesus Increases Self-worth Great Deal	Greatest Effort to Follow Jesus' Example	Religion Very Important
All 4 correct	46%	61%	60%	70%	56%
3 correct	4	3	6	7	5
2 correct	2	2	2	1	2
1 correct	2	2	2	1	2
None correct	3	2	4	3	4
Don't know	43	30	26	18	31
Total	100%	100%	100%	100%	100%

27. Knowledge of Jesus' Birthplace

The question: *Where was Jesus born?*

	All Respondents	Jesus Was God	Relation with Jesus Increases Self-worth Great Deal	Greatest Effort to Follow Jesus' Example	Religion Very Important
Bethlehem	70%	79%	82%	85%	78%
Incorrect	17	15	15	13	14
Miscellaneous	*	*	*	1	*
Don't know	13	6	3	1	8
Total	100%	100%	100%	100%	100%

*Less than one half of one percent

28. Ways Used to Nourish or Strengthen Faith

The question: *What sort of things, if any, do you do to nourish or strengthen your faith?*

	All Respond- ents	Jesus Was God	Relation with Jesus Increases Self-worth Great Deal	Greatest Effort to Follow Jesus' Example	Religion Very Import- ant
Pray by oneself	59%	73%	80%	74%	72%
Help others	51	60	67	65	59
Attend religious services	44	59	61	61	58
Read the Bible	39	54	62	68	54
Listen to sermons or lectures	36	48	54	56	47
Meditation	32	41	49	52	41
Take walks, seek to commune with nature	31	32	35	31	28
Receive Holy Communion	29	43	43	53	40
Watch religious TV programs	21	28	32	43	29
Read religious books other than the Bible	21	30	35	41	32
Pray in a group	19	27	34	41	28
Seek out fellow Christians	17	27	32	38	27
Praying with others for spiritual healing	14	22	26	39	21
Read religious magazines	13	21	23	36	21
Read the Bible in a group	12	17	22	29	18
Evangelize, encourage others to accept Jesus	11	18	22	33	18
Spiritual counseling	8	12	15	23	13
None of the above	6	2	1	—	1
Don't know	3	1	1	1	3

NOTE: Totals add to more than 100 because of multiple responses.

29. Feelings in Church or Synagogue

The question: *In church or synagogue, have you ever felt afraid of God, guilty as a sinner, close to God, or that you are a wonderful person?*

	All Respondents	Jesus Was God	Relation with Jesus Increases Self-worth Great Deal	Greatest Effort to Follow Jesus' Example	Religion Very Important
Afraid of God					
Yes	16%	21%	18%	16%	18%
No	78	77	80	83	78
Don't know	6	2	2	1	4
Total	100%	100%	100%	100%	100%
Guilty as a sinner					
Yes	52%	62%	62%	52%	60%
No	42	36	36	46	36
Don't know	6	2	2	2	4
Total	100%	100%	100%	100%	100%
Close to God					
Yes	80%	90%	95%	98%	93%
No	13	7	2	1	4
Don't know	7	3	3	1	3
Total	100%	100%	100%	100%	100%
That you are a wonderful person					
Yes	47%	48%	61%	65%	53%
No	40	42	30	26	36
Don't know	13	10	9	9	11
Total	100%	100%	100%	100%	100%

30. Attempts to Encourage Others to Believe in Jesus Christ

The question: *Have you ever tried to encourage someone to believe in Jesus Christ or to accept him as his or her Savior?*

	All Respondents	Jesus Was God	Relation with Jesus Increases Self-worth Great Deal	Greatest Effort to Follow Jesus' Example	Religion Very Important
Yes	51%	64%	80%	83%	69%
No	41	33	19	14	26
No opinion	8	3	1	3	5
Total	100%	100%	100%	100%	100%

31. Ways in Which Churches Can Better Serve

The question: *In which of these ways, if any, would you like to see churches better serve you?*

	All Respond-ents	Jesus Was God	Relation with Jesus Increases Self-worth Great Deal	Greatest Effort to Follow Jesus' Example	Religion Very Import-ant
Help you put your faith into practice	37%	47%	49%	51%	45%
Enable you to deepen your relationship with Jesus Christ	35	46	51	49	46
Shed light on issues such as the problem of suffering, death, and dying	33	37	37	33	35
Help people to be more effective parents	32	37	38	36	35
Enable you to serve others better	31	38	40	34	35
Develop greater use of your "gifts" or talents	21	26	26	32	22
Help you in your prayer life	19	25	29	30	25
Through counseling with prayer	16	21	23	26	22
Other	1	1	1	1	2
None	8	6	4	4	5
Don't know	14	6	6	9	10

NOTE: Totals add to more than 100 because of multiple responses.

32. Happiness/satisfaction Levels

The questions: *Would you say that you are very happy, fairly happy, or not too happy? Are you very satisfied with the way things are going in your life, fairly satisfied, or not too satisfied?*

	Very Happy	Very Satisfied
General Public	44%	45%
High Religiosity		
Highly spiritually committed	68	63
Attend church more than weekly	66	56
Very high Christian life	61	60
Member of evangelical denomination	59	53
Far right religious beliefs	57	56
Low Religiosity		
Very low Christian life	29	39
Very low spiritual commitment	30	36
No religious preference	31	38
Religion not important in life	32	33

33. Religious Commitment of College Students

The questions: *How important to you are your religious beliefs? How often do you attend religious services? Since you have been in college, has your religious commitment become much stronger, a little stronger, a little weaker, much weaker, is there?*

Importance of Religious Beliefs
Very important	50%
Fairly important	33
Not too important	11
Not at all important	3
No religious beliefs	3

Church/Synagogue Attendance
Every week	39
About once a month	19
A few times a year	21
Almost never	20

Change in Religious Commitment
Much stronger	15
A little stronger	20
A little weaker	11
Much weaker	5
No change	48

34. Ability to Tell Whether Someone Is a True Christian

The question: *Do you think you can usually tell if someone is a true Christian, even if you've only known him or her for a few minutes?*

	All Respondents	Jesus Was God	Relation with Jesus Increases Self-worth Great Deal	Greatest Effort to Follow Jesus' Example	Religion Very Important
Yes	31%	39%	46%	56%	38%
No	58	55	50	36	54
No opinion	11	6	4	8	8
Total	100%	100%	100%	100%	100%

35. Extent of Deepening of Relationship with Jesus

The question: *To what extent, if at all, do you feel that your relationship with Jesus is deepening—a great deal, somewhat, hardly at all, or not at all?* (Asked of those describing the degree of their effort to follow Jesus' example.)

	All Respondents	Greatest Possible Effort	Considerable Effort	Some Effort	Hardly Any or No Effort
A great deal	27%	79%	37%	13%	3%
Somewhat	44	18	56	58	22
Hardly at all	12	1	4	20	29
Not at all	8	*	2	6	42
No opinion	9	2	1	3	4
Total	100%	100%	100%	100%	100%

*Less than one half of one percent